More Praise for *Radical Product Thinking*

"Dutt's powerful methodology offers a step-by-step approach for building success-ful products that doubles as a guide to infusing meaning in everyday work and packing purpose into every organization. This book belongs on the shelf of every leader and innovator."
—**Daniel H. Pink, author of *Drive*, *When*, and *To Sell Is Human***

"In *Radical Product Thinking: The New Mindset for Innovating Smarter,* R. Dutt offers a compelling and important antidote to short-term thinking so prevalent in product design and especially in redesign. She highlights how tinkering with established products, ignoring opportunities in large-scale product reinvention in favor of immediate financial performance, is often a recipe for longer-term prod-uct misalignment and irrelevance. The book's concepts are explained well, and the examples are helpful and illuminating. A book whose message is both timely and timeless."
—**David Schmittlein, John C. Head III Dean and Professor of Marketing, MIT Sloan School of Management**

"R. Dutt offers a great methodical process for radical product innovation so you can avoid the trap of making incremental optimizations that lead to local, myopic maxima. If you are using Agile-like methodologies to harness the power of itera-tions and incremental development, you need *Radical Product Thinking* to stay mission-driven."
—**Giorgos Zacharia, President, Kayak**

"R. Dutt hits the nail on the head with *Radical Product Thinking,* because what drives our brightest young talent to join one company over another is often not money but a powerful vision that guides every project in the organization. This is a book for our times that will help managers not only compete for talent but also leapfrog competitors by creating novel products that capture customer attention and inspire."
—**Fernando F. Suarez, PhD, Jean C. Tempel Professor of Entrepreneurship and Innovation and Chair, Entrepreneurship and Innovation Group, Northeastern University**

"Dutt has written an insightful book on how you can change the world around you through your products. She offers refreshing perspectives on how a purpose-driven approach can make products that are truly transformative. Anyone making a product—from business leaders to entrepreneurs to policymakers—will find this book a useful guide."
—**Ravi Menon, Managing Director, Monetary Authority of Singapore**

RADICAL
PRODUCT
THINKING

R. DUTT

RADICAL PRODUCT THINKING

THE NEW MINDSET FOR INNOVATING SMARTER

BK®

Berrett–Koehler Publishers, Inc.

Berrett-Koehler Publishers, Inc.
1333 Broadway, Suite 1000
Oakland, CA 94612-1921
Tel: (510) 817-2277
Fax: (510) 817-2278
www.bkconnection.com

ORDERING INFORMATION

Quantity sales. Special discounts are available on quantity purchases by corporations, associations, and others. For details, contact the "Special Sales Department" at the Berrett-Koehler address above.
Individual sales. Berrett-Koehler publications are available through most bookstores. They can also be ordered directly from Berrett-Koehler: Tel: (800) 929-2929; Fax: (802) 864-7626; www.bkconnection.com.
Orders for college textbook / course adoption use. Please contact Berrett-Koehler: Tel: (800) 929-2929; Fax: (802) 864-7626.

Distributed to the U.S. trade and internationally by Penguin Random House Publisher Services.

Berrett-Koehler and the BK logo are registered trademarks of Berrett-Koehler Publishers, Inc.

Printed in the United States of America

Berrett-Koehler books are printed on long-lasting acid-free paper. When it is available, we choose paper that has been manufactured by environmentally responsible processes. These may include using trees grown in sustainable forests, incorporating recycled paper, minimizing chlorine in bleaching, or recycling the energy produced at the paper mill.

Library of Congress Cataloging-in-Publication Data

Names: Dutt, R. (Radhika), author.
Title: Radical product thinking : the new mindset for innovating smarter / R. Dutt.
Description: First edition. | Oakland, CA : Berrett-Koehler Publishers, Inc., [2021] | Includes bibliographical references and index. | Summary: "Iteration rules product development, but it isn't enough to produce dramatic results. This book champions Radical Product Thinking, a systematic methodology for building visionary, game-changing products"-- Provided by publisher.
Identifiers: LCCN 2021022007 (print) | LCCN 2021022008 (ebook) | ISBN 9781523093311 (paperback) | ISBN 9781523093328 (adobe pdf) | ISBN 9781523093335 (epub)
Subjects: LCSH: New products. | Product design. | Creative thinking. | Strategic planning.
Classification: LCC HF5415.153 .D88 2021 (print) | LCC HF5415.153 (ebook) | DDC 658.5/75--dc23
LC record available at https://lccn.loc.gov/2021022007
LC ebook record available at https://lccn.loc.gov/2021022008

First Edition
26 25 24 23 22 21   10 9 8 7 6 5 4 3 2 1

Cover designer: Adam Johnson
Book editor: PeopleSpeak
Interior designer: Reider Books

To Arya and Rishi,
May you change the world in ways that inspire you, big or small.
You've already changed mine.

CONTENTS

INTRODUCTION

A Repeatable Model for Building World-Changing Products

For more than a century, building world-changing products seemed to be reserved for a small group of visionaries, such as Henry Ford, Steve Jobs, Bill Gates, and Richard Branson. These leaders were lionized for being able to set monumental goals and knowing just how to achieve them—they seemed to have an innate gift for being vision-driven.

It was clear that to succeed at building world-changing products, these leaders had a vision—most organizations have learned from this and have vision statements. Yet taking an idea from concept to reality seems elusively difficult, and only a few organizations (and individuals) seem to have a knack for delivering visionary products.

Despite knowing that it's important to be vision-driven, it's easy to default to being iteration-led. If you've ever experienced being iteration-led in an organization, you know that it feels like you're tinkering and focusing on the short term but ultimately missing out on the large-scale opportunity. It turns out that a vision alone isn't enough to be vision-driven—it requires a new mindset.

To understand the difference between vision-driven and iteration-led, consider the development of the 737 MAX, which had to be grounded worldwide in March 2019 after two newly delivered airplanes crashed within five months, killing 346 people.

Boeing's 737 platform first entered airline service in 1968. After 40 years of iterations on the 737, engineers at Boeing knew that the plane was nearing the end of its life span. Its low frame, which was a highly desirable feature in the early days of manual loading and unloading of cargo, was now limiting the size of the engine that could fit under the wings. Even in the '90s, Boeing had to make increasingly desperate attempts to fit larger engines on the 737—the engine in the Next Generation series, for example, had to be egg-shaped to fit under the low frame.[1]

At this point, Boeing could have pursued a long-term vision and committed to designing a completely new airplane to replace the 737. But on the heels of having invested billions in research and development to develop the new Dreamliner, it was tempting to keep milking the 737 cash cow, Boeing's bestseller since the '70s. Boeing management delayed addressing the market demand for a new narrow-body aircraft.

In 2010, archrival Airbus filled this void with the A320neo, which offered 20 percent better fuel efficiency. When American Airlines, Boeing's biggest and most important customer, decided to add the A320neo to its fleet, Boeing had to act fast. In August 2011, Boeing decided to create the 737 MAX by iterating on the existing 737 platform. While engineers rolled their eyes at having to upgrade the 737 yet again, it seemed to address Boeing's short-term business goals. This iteration would allow Boeing to launch a certified product in roughly half the time and at 10–15 percent of the cost of designing a new plane from scratch.[2]

But giving the 737 larger and stronger engines wasn't a simple task. The 737's low frame required engineers to move the engine forward. Unfortunately, this caused the plane to become dynamically unstable—its nose tended to tip upward, which made it prone to stalling. To get around this, Boeing developed an automated anti-stall system, the Maneuvering Characteristics Augmentation System (MCAS), to point the noise downward when the plane risked stalling. Ultimately, the MCAS was blamed for both the Lion Air and Ethiopian Airlines crashes that resulted in 346 fatalities.

Boeing had allowed market pressures to drive an iteration-led approach to product development. In building the 737 MAX, it had found what is referred to as a *local maximum*, a solution that optimized for the short term by preventing the loss of marquee clients to Airbus. In the process, however, Boeing had lost its focus on its most important mission: building safe and reliable aircraft. What Boeing needed instead was a vision-driven approach of investing in a brand new plane to reach what's called the *global maximum*, the optimal solution in the long term for Boeing, its passengers, and the airlines.

Finding a local maximum is like finding the best move while looking at only a few pieces on the chessboard that are under attack. In contrast, finding the global maximum means playing the long game to find the best move over the entire chessboard. This requires a vision for what you want to achieve and a plan for getting there.

Boeing wasn't vision-driven, although it had a vision statement. An iteration-led approach often takes root in a vision that's broad and driven by business goals, for example, "to be the best in . . ." or "to revolutionize . . ." In its *2018 Annual Report*, Boeing stated, "Our purpose and mission is to connect, protect, explore and inspire the world through aerospace innovation. We aspire to be the best in aerospace and an enduring global industrial champion."[3] A purpose defined this broadly is the equivalent of going on a road trip and stating your destination is "To go north and have the best road trip."

Without being able to picture your destination in the long term, your short-term needs are the most visible and determine your direction. Not only did Boeing focus on short-term financial results by iterating on the 737 platform over decades, it also optimized for short-term gains by spending $43 billion on share buybacks from 2013 until the first quarter of 2019.[4] To put these figures in perspective, consider that to build the Dreamliner from scratch, Boeing invested $32 billion over eight years. A broad vision of having the best road trip can lead to a myopic focus.

For years, however, we had learned that starting with a broad and aspirational vision was key to building successful products and companies. We've even accepted and normalized the myopic focus on the short term that often accompanies this approach. Research shows that since the 1980s, companies on average are becoming more short-term oriented.[5] As the time horizon for organizational planning shrinks, companies increasingly seek investment opportunities that yield short-term returns—they find local maxima.

General Electric's vision, "Become the number one or number two in every market we serve," was heralded as exemplary. Soon after he became CEO, Jack Welch gave a speech titled "Growing Fast in a Slow Growth Economy" in which he said, "GE would be the locomotive pulling the GDP and not the caboose following it." In the speech he laid out GE's plan for consistently growing profits by either fixing or selling businesses that weren't attaining the goal of being number one or two. His speech was hugely influential in shifting management styles toward short-term performance.[6]

Under Welch, GE's revenues grew from $25 billion in 1981 when he inherited it to $130 billion in 2001 when he retired. Unfortunately, this phenomenal growth was largely driven by short-termism.

Quarter after quarter, to consistently meet analysts growth expectations, Welch often used growth from GE Capital to compensate for weak results in other parts of the business. Before Welch took the helm in 1981, GE Capital made up only 6 percent of GE's net profits. By 1990, it had steadily increased to 24 percent.[7]

In 1991, GE became the largest company by market capitalization—the stock market was giving loud feedback that GE's road trip was going well.[8] By the time Welch retired in 2001, GE had announced 101 consecutive quarters of growth and GE Capital had contributed to 42 percent of GE's profits.

Welch's successor, Jeffrey Immelt, did his best to continue the streak. In the financial downturn after 9/11, GE Capital's contributions toward overall profitability became increasingly important. To continue growing GE Capital, in 2004, with the housing market booming, GE bought what seemed like an innovative company, WMC, for $500 million. WMC was the sixth largest subprime lender and dealt in something called mortgage-backed securities.

In 2007, GE lost $1 billion as a result of the subprime mortgage loan crisis and was later required to pay a penalty of $1.5 billion by the Department of Justice for its role in the financial crisis. The fallout from the subprime crisis continued to haunt GE for more than a decade afterward, until GE settled the case with the DOJ and sold off most of GE Capital's portfolio.

The vision of becoming number one or number two in every market meant GE was on a road trip without a clear destination. Even the markets were confused about GE's core offering—in 2005 they recategorized GE from a manufacturing company to a financial services company. The iteration-led approach led the company we know for bringing us the lightbulb to expand into lending subprime mortgages.

Applying the iteration-led approach in our organizations means that products often don't reach their full potential. They tend to become bloated, fragmented, directionless, and driven by the wrong metrics.

Occasionally, however, an iteration-led company strikes gold with a local maximum, and each such financial success further entrenches this model in our business practices. The birth of Twitter is one such example.

Twitter started as Odeo, a podcasting company that was founded in 2005. But in the fall of that year, when Apple announced iTunes with a built-in podcasting platform, it was clear that Odeo's days were numbered. As the founders solicited employees for new business ideas, Jack Dorsey, an engineer at Odeo, shared his idea for a platform where people could share status updates with groups. Twitter as a microblogging platform evolved from iterations of this idea that performed well with users. Twitter was a local maximum created in response to Odeo's imminent failure and happened to strike gold.[9]

Stories of iteration-led successes are fun to read, but for every product that becomes a financial success by applying an iterative approach, there's a graveyard of failures that never get media attention.

I've fallen into the trap of being iteration-led myself. The economy was on an upswing during the dot-com bubble when I cofounded my first startup, Lobby7, in 2000. Our vision was to "revolutionize wireless," and we started building wireless applications for phones and personal digital assistants (remember PDAs like the PalmPilot?) that could be connected over Wi-Fi. We were a services company, so we could explore the needs of many different industry verticals until we found a "killer app." We'd then pivot into a product company to focus on that killer app. In today's language, our plan was to iterate until we found a product-market fit.

On our road trip of building wireless apps for clients, we realized that the lack of keyboards or touch screens on phones made any app very hard to use. You had to type each letter slowly by using the number pad. Being a group of smart technologists, we asked, "What if you could interact with your device using voice and text interchangeably?" This was a hard problem to solve at the time as devices didn't have enough computing power for voice recognition. But we overcame the hurdles and enabled voice recognition on phones as our main product—an early version of Siri.

Like many other startups with funding, we iterated on different products and business models to see what worked. In the end, we developed an interesting technology, but we didn't survive the downturn— our iterations had burnt through the funding we had, and Lobby7 was acquired for the technology.

I didn't get rich at Lobby7, but I left with a priceless education.

After brief stints at two other startups that were similarly iteration-led, I landed at the broadcast division of Avid Technology in 2003. There I got to experience a very different strategy for building products.

Avid at the time was well-known in the Hollywood movie studios; practically every movie nominated for an Oscar had been edited on an Avid Media Composer. Now Avid was trying to break into the broadcast news market, dominated by Sony. Television news stories in 2003 were still filmed on tape (mostly Sony's) and then edited for broadcast on Sony editing machines. David Schleifer, the head of Avid Broadcast, had a vision for how a completely digital newsroom could transform TV news production.

While editing a story, production crews needed to find older news stories that were related and then edit in relevant excerpts to add context and impact. But it was hard to access videotape that had been created by other teams, find the exact clips you wanted, and integrate them into a new piece. While most of our competitors replicated the tape-based workflow in a digital format, we set out to build a digital product suite that offered a completely new and vastly easier workflow. David believed that if we made our offering irresistible, broadcasters would give up on tape altogether.

We built our product suite incrementally, adding a new component roughly every year: Avid Unity for storing data storage, Avid Media Manager for finding and sharing video, Avid Airspeed for preparing the stories for transmission. Our development was steady and deliberate, with no dramatic pivots. Instead of repeating a memorable slogan for a vision statement, we were driven by a clear understanding of the problem we had set out to solve.

The only downside was that we often felt that Avid wasn't investing aggressively enough in our work. To complement our limited engineering resources, we partnered with customers—those who saw the value of a completely new digital workflow and were willing to pay extra so we could add additional features. My role at Avid was to work closely with customers to understand their workflow needs and identify gaps in our product suite. Where needed, we would build additional functionality to fill those gaps. In essence, our customers became our incremental R&D function.

Without a clear vision, however, this strategy could have easily gone awry by leading us to add niche features that only one customer would want. Had we offered 100 percent customized features for each customer, we would have found local maxima through increased sales, but this approach would have been a huge distraction from our overall product development. And ultimately, it wouldn't have been good for customers either, because customized products wouldn't be sustainable in the long run. Instead, we helped our customers buy into our vision of a digital workflow that solved the inefficiencies of tape to transform TV news production.

Within five years Avid dominated the broadcast market, with nearly every major TV news organization (including NBC, CBS, and ABC in the United States; CBC in Canada; BBC and ITV in the United Kingdom) using Avid's suite of products. David Schleifer's vision-driven strategy had worked.

I found it interesting that the success of that strategy showed even in our social interactions. At Avid, any drinks night or party would lead to passionate but friendly debates over our products and management decisions. Years later, when ex–Avid employees get together, we still talk just as passionately about the company. At Lobby7, on the other hand, whenever the staff got together socially, we didn't talk much about work—in being iteration-led we didn't share a deep conviction of purpose.

To be clear, my criticism of being iteration-led is not intended to dismiss the importance of iteration. In the last decade, we've learned to innovate faster by testing ideas in the market to discover what customers want and then refining our products through feedback-driven iteration—we've learned to harness the power of iteration. Until now, however, we haven't had a methodology to guide us to be more vision-driven. The result is that our ability to iterate has given us a faster car for this road trip, but our ability to set the destination and navigate to it hasn't kept pace.

If your vision is as broad as "to go north and have the best road trip," your feedback-driven iterations could take you to Boston or lead you to Toronto. Taking a vision-driven approach means your vision drives your iterations so you end up where you intended to.

To date, the road to being vision-driven has been foggy. Much of the conventional wisdom that a good vision must be aspirational and a BHAG (Big Hairy Audacious Goal) has often led us astray. To build vision-driven products, it's not enough to have just *any* vision. We need a radical approach to crafting a vision.

Once we have a good vision, we then need to translate it systematically into our everyday actions. Our short-term business needs often compete for attention as we work toward the long-term—along the way, it's easy to be tempted to settle for a local maximum and lose sight of the global maximum. We need a practical approach to stay vision-driven once we craft a vision.

Radical Product Thinking helps you build the mindset you need to systematically build vision-driven products and innovate smarter.

My path to product leadership helped me realize that we can all apply product thinking and take a methodical approach to build products, irrespective of our role and industry. I've built products in media and entertainment, advertising technology, research, government, public art, robotics, and wine to name a few. In fact, every job I've ever taken has been in a new industry. The roles I've held have been equally varied, including marketing, strategy, project management, operations, and CEO. This diverse experience has made me realize that "product" is a way of thinking, not a job title or function. Whether you work in a nonprofit, a government organization, a service provider, research, a high-tech startup, or freelancing, you have a product. Our traditional view of a product as a physical or virtual object is outdated.

Radical Product Thinking (RPT) means finding the global maximum by thinking about the change you want to see in the world. Your product then is an improvable system to bring about that change. In RPT your product is led by the vision for the change it's intended to create. A radical product is vision-driven and has a clear reason for being, which drives strategy, prioritization, and execution. RPT offers organizations a clear guide to developing this mindset so each of us can build vision-driven products.

This book is structured in three parts. The examples in the introduction raise awareness of the drawbacks of being iteration-led and make the case for a new way of creating world-changing products. Part I explains how vision-driven products create transformative change and helps you recognize the need for Radical Product Thinking in your own organization. Chapter 1 illustrates how vision-driven products can be built systematically to change the world and introduces the RPT approach. In chapter 2 we'll build a common vocabulary so we can explore the barriers, or "diseases," that get in the way of great products. Reading about these diseases will help you diagnose the areas that need the most attention so you can begin to build successful, vision-driven products.

Part II of the book gives you easy and practical steps to apply this approach and spread this thinking across an organization. In chapters 3–7, you'll start to get good at using the five elements of RPT—vision, strategy, prioritization, execution and measurement, and culture.

Each of these chapters is designed to give you one practical tool— you could use any one of these tools by itself and start reaping the benefits. In fact, you may find it helpful to read through the entire book first before picking the tools that you think would be most beneficial and then work through the exercises one chapter at a time. While the chapters are organized linearly, your process of working through the exercises doesn't have to be. As you develop your strategy, for example, you may realize that you need to go back and edit your vision.

The chapters contain the templates you need. But to make it easier to flip back and forth as you work through the exercises, you may want to print out the tool kit and use it alongside the book when you're ready to do the exercises. You can download the printable tool kit for free from the RadicalProduct.com website.

The exercises are intended to help you apply RPT on a regular basis until these skills become muscle memory. At that point you'll be able to apply this thinking intuitively and help your colleagues do the same.

Part III of the book explains the responsibility that comes with the superpower of building vision-driven products. Chapter 8 explains the concept of "digital pollution" and the unintended consequences of our products on society. Chapter 9 introduces the Hippocratic Oath of Product and how you can embrace the responsibility that comes with building successful products.

The book concludes with examples that will inspire you to apply this philosophy to any activity through which you want to create change. Creating world-changing products doesn't have to be reserved for rare, visionary leaders—each of us can engineer change through vision-driven products.

I myself have applied Radical Product Thinking in the process of writing this book: it's a product designed to create change. My goal is to make it easier for you to build dramatically better products that help you bring the world a little closer to the world you want to live in. I look forward to guiding you on this journey because your success will be the main metric for my own success.

PART I

INNOVATING SMARTER REQUIRES A NEW MINDSET

CHAPTER 1

WHY WE NEED RADICAL PRODUCT THINKING

A vision-driven product begins with a clear picture of the change you want to bring to the world. This vision must then permeate every aspect of the product's design.

For a great case study on how a vision-driven product is fundamentally different from an iteration-led one, consider the comparison between Tesla's Model 3 and GM's Chevy Bolt. Sandy Munro, a well-known automotive expert, shared a detailed comparison of the Model 3 and the Bolt after taking apart the two cars and painstakingly analyzing each component. Munro summarizes his findings in an *Autoline After Hours* interview, describing the Bolt as a "good car." But he was far more excited by the Model 3. "Tesla has the best design for electronics, the best harness design, the best driving experience, the best motor. . . . Everything apart from the skin is brilliant." His only criticism of the Model 3 was the body—an area where Tesla has admitted to having problems.

Munro gives an example of Tesla's vision-driven innovation: a smaller, cheaper, and more powerful engine. He says he had heard about the Hall effect in electric motors, which can make the motor 40 percent faster, but had never seen it used in electric vehicle (EV) engines. In his teardown comparisons to date, Tesla was the only carmaker using the Hall effect for its engine. It required Tesla to invent a new manufacturing process to glue together magnets of opposing polarity under high stress. Munro had never seen anything like Tesla's magnets before and couldn't figure out how anyone could mass-produce them.

Compare that to his description of the approach GM took to build the Bolt: "GM doesn't have a lot of money to spend on designing every vehicle from scratch. So they started with a Spark chassis, outsourced the battery, and got a car to market quickly." GM was iteration-led and found a local maximum in the Bolt.

The difference between how Tesla and GM approached the race to build commercially viable electric cars is evident in the vision behind these two cars. Tesla's Model 3 was driven by a radical vision of building an affordable car that didn't require a compromise from the driver to go "green." When GM designed the Chevy Bolt, it was driven by the vision of beating the Tesla Model 3 to market with an EV that would have a range of more than 200 miles between charges.

Tesla designed the Model 3 as a mechanism to create the change it wanted to bring to the world (accelerating the transition to electric cars by making them more affordable)—that's Radical Product Thinking. This clear purpose was translated into every aspect of the car. One team designed a more efficient electric motor using the Hall effect; another designed a new magnet with varying polarities; another figured out a process to manufacture this innovative magnet. The connection across these roles and tactical activities is that the teams were all thinking about a radical product, driven by a common vision. As Munro summarized his view on the Model 3, "This car is totally different. This is not inching up. This is revolutionary."

Thinking radically about a product is often reflected in the organization's structure. Take the cooling system in the Model 3, a single system that cools the entire car, including the batteries, cabin, and motor. It was designed as a single system to be as efficient as possible. In the Bolt, as in traditional cars, separate systems cool the different areas of the car. As Munro points out, at GM, each of these systems is someone's domain and fiefdom.[1] While creating a single cooling system has been talked about a lot in Detroit, it would require "crossing over too many lines." At Tesla, the radical vision transcended organizational boundaries.

GM was able to find local maxima—it got a new model to market quickly, and it was a pretty good car at a lower price point. But Tesla found the global maximum, a breakthrough vehicle that has been outselling the Mercedes C-Class, BMW 3 Series, and Audi A4 combined.[2]

Tesla used iterations to *refine* how to get where it was going. Tesla's first iteration, the Roadster, ran on battery packs made of 6,831 off-the-shelf lithium-ion cells used in laptop batteries. Today Tesla's Model 3 battery packs contain cells that were developed by the company with Panasonic. Munro views Tesla's batteries as the best among the EVs—they provide the longest range and fastest charging times while occupying the least space. The company continues to iterate on its product. Tesla has acknowledged issues in manufacturing the Model 3 and continues to improve the design of the body and manufacturing processes.

GM, in contrast, used iterations to *define* where it was going. By starting with the same chassis as the Spark, even the same layout of the engine in the front, GM was preserving what it knew best (gasoline cars) and guaranteed that the Bolt would be evolutionary but not revolutionary.

"But wait," you might say, "Tesla had a lead on EVs. Given more time (and iterations), wouldn't GM have found the same global maximum that Tesla found?" Fortunately, we can use historical evidence to answer this question: coming up with a visionary solution wasn't a matter of iterating for long enough. It turns out GM had launched its first electric vehicle, the EV1, in 1996, well before Tesla was conceived.

GM leased the EV1 as a market test to customers in California, who loved the product. In fact, when GM wanted to shut down the program, citing liability issues and discontinuation of parts, customers sent checks to GM asking to buy their leased cars at zero risk to the company. GM didn't even have to commit to servicing the cars—their owners wanted to keep using them regardless! GM returned the checks and chose to shut down the product line because an electric car has fewer moving parts and requires fewer parts to be replaced in the car's lifetime—the EV1 would have cannibalized GM's spare parts business.[3]

While GM had come up with an EV well before Tesla, their iterations weren't vision-driven and it settled for the local maximum. Ironically, GM's cancellation of the EV1 program led Elon Musk to start Tesla and eventually build the visionary Model 3.

Despite their shortcomings, local maxima are often tempting because they can help you optimize for your corner of the chessboard. They can help you maximize profitability and business goals in the near term, as GM did by scuttling its EV program.

Since the 1980s the ideology of shareholder primacy, where a company's primary goal is to maximize shareholder value, has become entrenched in business culture.[4] Academics argued that managers would best serve companies (and society) by working to maximize shareholder value. Often this means delivering financial results every quarter to meet shareholders' expectations of profits and growth—you're incentivized to optimize for just a few pieces on the chessboard.

Startups too have similar incentives for a short-term focus. To demonstrate progress to investors and raise your next round of funding, you need to show quick results in terms of financial metrics or key performance indicators (KPIs), for example, the number of users, revenues, and growth. Irrespective of the size of the organization, the success of a product is typically measured on a single dimension: financial KPI.

The book *Lean Startup* taught us to innovate faster by testing things in the market, seeing what works, and iterating. But to assess what's working, we almost always look to financial metrics, typically usage or revenues. Don't know whether customers want the feature you have in mind? Launch it and let the usage data drive your decision. An iteration-led approach can move financial KPI up and to the right, but it doesn't guarantee that you'll build game-changing products. On the chessboard, optimizing for capturing a few pieces doesn't guarantee that you'll win the game.

Ironically, I've found that the pure pursuit of financial metrics often gets in the way of building successful products. When *Lean Startup* was published in 2011, it promised to democratize innovation. In a growing economy where credit was plentiful, the movement popularized the phrase "Fail fast, learn fast," in the tech industry. It emphasized launching a minimum viable product (MVP) to test and refine an offering instead of spending time on an elaborate business plan. The Lean approach is typically paired with Agile, a development methodology for building products incrementally and incorporating feedback throughout the development process. Especially when Lean and Agile are used together, it creates the illusion that you don't need to start with a clear vision—you could discover your vision along the way.

The problem with discovering your vision along the way is illustrated by the dialog between Alice and the Cheshire Cat in Lewis Carroll's *Alice's Adventures in Wonderland*:

> "Would you tell me, please, which way I ought to go from here?"
>
> "That depends a good deal on where you want to get to," said the Cat.
>
> "I don't much care where—" said Alice.
>
> "Then it doesn't matter which way you go," said the Cat.[5]

In discovering your vision along the way, your product can become a sailboat at sea without a North Star—you go wherever the currents and KPIs take you. As a business leader, you experience many strong forces pushing you in different directions. Your investors may see a trend that you're not capitalizing on, a board member may share an idea (because he sat next to another CEO on a plane who "knew" just what your company should be doing), and different customers may be asking for different things. Without a clear vision and strategy to drive the ideas you test and iteratively improve, many good products go bad as they meander and lose their way.

To be clear, this is not to dismiss Lean Startup. Lean and Agile are both excellent methodologies that I still use and highly recommend for feedback-driven execution. Lean and Agile give you speed, helping you get to your destination faster. However, they don't tell you *where* you need to go.

Over the years, through my work in different industries and types of organizations from startups to government agencies, I've found the same pattern of mistakes as we build and scale our products and companies using iteration-led approaches to pursue local maxima. I was sharing my learnings and frustrations about product development with two ex-colleagues, Geordie Kaytes and Nidhi Aggarwal. Though they came from different backgrounds, they echoed my frustrations—both had also learned to build products through trial and error. Kaytes was a UX (user experience) strategist at Fresh Tilled Soil, a design agency in Boston, while Aggarwal had founded QwikLABS (acquired by Google) and was later the COO at Tamr, a machine learning startup. Among the three of us, we had built innumerable products over the years, and we saw the need for a methodical approach for building successful, vision-driven products. We realized that we must look at products differently.

We found that without a methodology to do this, organizations commonly use Lean and Agile execution to fill the gap. Using these methodologies while measuring success on the single dimension of financial metrics made it easier to find the local maxima but miss out on the global maximum. We cataloged the most common barriers that have repeatedly gotten in the way of building great products as a result of this approach. We spoke with people in diverse functions, industries, and countries who all faced similar problems.

We began to call these barriers *diseases* because they are contagious, damaging, and difficult to cure. These diseases are common because it's easy to make mistakes at every step of product development.

We worked on translating what we had learned the hard way into a systematic process that anyone could apply. We drew insights from large and small businesses, nonprofits, and governments, and we organized them into a clear, repeatable process. We then tested and refined this process by working with individuals and teams in a range of organizations around the world, including early-stage high-tech startups, companies offering professional services, social enterprises, nonprofits, and research organizations. The result is what we call Radical Product Thinking.

The word *radical* can sound overwhelming, but the *Oxford English Dictionary* defines it as "relating to or affecting the fundamental nature of something (especially of change or action); far-reaching or thorough."[6] *Radical* in reference to medical treatment means thorough and intended to be completely curative.

Radical Product Thinking means being inspired by a change you want to bring to the world and thinking about your product comprehensively as a mechanism for creating that change. We've designed our Radical Product Tool Kit as a clear, repeatable methodology for creating game-changing products—step by step from envisioning a change to translating your vision into daily activities to delivering a final product. RPT will also give your team a shared language that makes communication easier and helps you bring others on your journey.

Here are the three pillars of the RPT philosophy:

1. *Think of your product as your mechanism for creating change:* The change you are working to bring to the world isn't necessarily through a high-tech product. It could be through the work of your nonprofit, the research you're conducting, or the freelance services you're offering. Any of these could be your product if it's your mechanism to bring change. Consequently,

you can apply the RPT approach to any product you're building to create change more effectively.

2. *Envision the change you want to bring to the world before engineering your product:* A product does not justify itself—it exists only to create your desired change and is successful only if it helps you achieve the end state you pictured. You can build the right product and evaluate it only if you know the impact you want to have. Without knowing the desired impact, it's difficult to recognize and address the unintended consequences your product may have.

3. *Create change by connecting your vision to your day-to-day activities:* A focus on execution feels satisfying—it feels like being on a galloping horse (even if it's galloping in the wrong direction). The RPT approach helps you connect your vision for change to your day-to-day activities so you can engineer that change systematically.

Table 1 presents a summary of the fundamental differences between an iteration-led approach and the RPT way.

SINGAPORE AS A
RADICAL PRODUCT

Singapore's history and economic transformation illustrate why Radical Product Thinking is a powerful model for creating change.

In 1854 the *Singapore Free Press* described Singapore as a small island filled with the "very dregs of the population of southeastern Asia."[7] Singapore had become a major port as a British colony, but the population was mostly poor and uneducated. Prostitution, gambling, and drug abuse were widespread, cholera and smallpox took their toll in overcrowded areas, and most people had no access to public health services. After World War II, Singapore chose to merge with Malaysia in 1963.

TABLE 1. Differences between an iteration-led approach and RPT

Iteration-led	RPT
This approach works for an evolutionary product when you're making small changes to an existing product or process.	RPT is needed for a game-changing product when you're creating a transformative change.
The vision is driven by business goals.	The vision is driven by the change you want to see.
The vision changes based on iterations, and iterations determine *where* you need to go next.	The vision rarely changes—iterations help you refine *how* to get where you want to go.
This approach helps you react to the situation you're in to find local maxima. You optimize for a few pieces on the chessboard that are under attack.	RPT helps you pursue the global maximum purposefully. You know the end goal and you play the long game in finding the best move across the chessboard.
The resulting product can easily become bloated and unfocused over time, as common product diseases creep in.	The resulting product is more likely to stay true to its original vision and purpose. Product diseases are less likely.
This approach contributes to digital pollution as iterations may create unintended consequences in society.	RPT helps you embrace the responsibility that comes with the power of building successful products that affect people.

At the time, it didn't seem like being an independent country was a realistic option. Singapore's future looked uncertain—it faced mass unemployment and housing shortages and lacked natural resources such as petroleum. It was a small island that even depended on Malaysia for its drinking water. It wasn't clear that such a country would survive.

Even the first prime minister of Singapore, Lee Kuan Yew, believed that Singapore's place in the world was as part of Malaysia. But after violent race riots in 1964, the government acknowledged that the merger had failed. Singapore hesitantly became an independent country in 1965. In the first press conference after independence, an emotional Lee said, "For me, it is a moment of anguish because all my life . . . you see, the whole of my adult life . . . I have believed in the Merger and the unity of these two territories. You know, it's a people, connected by geography, economics, and ties of kinship."[8]

But Singapore's history and the failed merger helped Lee formulate a clear picture of the impact he wanted to create for Singaporeans. In a different press conference, he described the world he wanted to create: "I have a few million people's lives to account for. And Singapore will survive, will trade with the whole world and will remain non-communist." Having experienced race riots while being part of Malaysia, Lee wanted to create equality among races. "There will be no race riots in Singapore. Never!"[9]

In an interview with the *International Herald Tribune* (excerpted in the *New York Times*) in 2007, he described that his mechanism to bring about the change he envisioned was to produce "a first world oasis in a third world region. So not only will [companies] come here to set up plants and manufacture, they will also come here and from here explore the region." His vision was to create a platform for businesses to explore Asia.

In the same interview, Lee described his strategy for developing a "first world oasis." Singapore needed to address the needs of Western businesses to make the island feel like home. The city needed to be green, be clean, and speak the same language (English). "We knew that if we were just like our neighbors, we would die. Because we've got nothing to offer against what they have to offer. So we had to produce something which is different and better than what they have. It's incorrupt. It's efficient. It's meritocratic. It works."[10] It's striking that he spoke as if he was building a product. Radical Product Thinking wasn't a thing in the '60s, but Lee had intuited this approach to systematically designing a product to create change.

The initiatives to arrive at these changes were carefully planned out and prioritized. For example, Singapore today is known for its cleanliness; in the West, we attribute this to the country's strict rules and the threat of punishment for littering. But logistically, if the majority weren't bought into the vision, enforcement would be very difficult. To achieve compliance from the population, the strategy has always been to persuade the majority through education campaigns and only then could fines and punishments be enforced for the willful minority.[11] For a clean Singapore, the country had to first conduct an education campaign on why cleanliness was important to achieve the vision before fines could be instituted. Every element of the strategy, from cleanliness to making English the common language, had to be translated into a prioritized set of activities.

When we look at our product as a means to get us to our destination, we become open to the possibility of constantly improving our mechanism for getting there. This is where iteration fits in. Iteration allows for a feedback-driven approach to executing on a clear vision and strategy. In the 2007 interview, Lee shared how he used iteration: "We are pragmatists. We don't stick to any ideology. Does it work? Let's try it and if it does work, fine, let's continue it. If it doesn't work, toss it out, try another one. We are not enamored with any ideology."[12] The administration's iterations were driven by a clear vision and strategy, but when an iteration proved that the underlying vision or strategy was flawed, the government corrected for it.

An example of iterative execution was Singapore's approach to public transport. The vision for public transport was clear—to have an inexpensive and extensive public transport system that accommodated a growing population. In 1995 Singapore privatized public transport in an effort to increase efficiency and improve pricing through competition. While this strategy seemed reasonable, it turned out that SMRT, the corporate entity managing public transport, was prioritizing short-term earnings because it was a publicly listed company. Trains became plagued by delays and safety incidents as railway maintenance and long-term investment were neglected for years. When it was clear that the privatization strategy wasn't achieving the vision for Singapore's public transport, the government changed its approach. SMRT was bought out by Temasek (a government investment arm) and delisted. Today Singapore's urban transportation is among the best globally and was ranked number one by McKinsey & Company in 2018.[13]

Lee led the Singaporean government when its challenge was to create a better life for the citizens of an impoverished island—he built a radical product and pursued the global maximum. Lee even used the analogy of playing a game of chess. "Some people play draughts—you eat one piece at a time. The affairs of men and nations are not that simple. This is a complicated business of chess."[14]

Today's administration faces a new challenge: the growing wealth inequality and balancing resource redistribution while living in the reality of a competitive, globalized economy. Beyond Singapore's miraculous transformation, Lee's visionary contribution was instilling a vision-driven product thinking approach in the government so the country could similarly engineer solutions to different challenges it would face in the future.

You can still see this approach permeating across the government agencies in Singapore. Every ministry or government organization has its own vision for the impact that it is working to create, and each has its corresponding product. Walk into any government organization and you'll see its vision clearly posted on a wall, and the service you experience matches it. At the end of your interaction, you are typically surveyed for feedback on your experience to constantly improve the product.

Here's my first experience of product thinking in a Singaporean government office. I arrived in Singapore with my family, and the very next day we went to the Ministry of Manpower's Employment Pass Services Center (EPSC) to get work permit cards. I was bracing myself for a long and painful experience as we headed there with two jet-lagged kids who had been up since two o'clock that morning.

Instead, we had an overwhelmingly positive experience that started with us walking into an office that looked more calming than most therapists' lobbies. During the short wait, we perused signs around the office that described the EPSC's design goals in crafting the customer experience: "Giving you certainty and control," "Keeping your different needs in mind," and "Being personable." The experience was true to these design goals, for example, our jet-lagged kids were happy in the cozy kids' zone, and when it was our turn we were called by name rather than a number. The staff took our pictures for the pass (we didn't have to find a photo booth), and they even gave each of us the opportunity to review our photo and decide if we wanted to have it retaken! And just like that, our work at the EPSC was done and the work permits would be mailed to us.

Issuing work permits is EPSC's "product," and this product is aligned with the vision articulated on the Ministry of Manpower's website. Here's an excerpt:

> We aim to develop a great workforce and a great workplace. Singaporeans can aspire to real income growth, fulfilling careers and financial security, while we maintain a manpower-lean and competitive economy.
>
> To achieve our vision and mission, we aim to enable companies to provide good jobs and Singaporeans to take up good jobs, to build a strong Singaporean core.
>
> We will maintain a skilled foreign workforce to complement our local workforce.[15]

To achieve this vision, Singapore needs to attract a skilled, diverse, foreign workforce. These workers fill a crucial gap in the labor force given the aging local population, hence the design goals that make working in Singapore easy for this group.

Lee's product was a "first world oasis"; EPSC's product was issuing work permits. Every level in an organization can apply Radical Product Thinking and create an impact through its product. At a more granular level, each person in an organization contributes a unique product. The impact created by the organization is the collective impact of each of these products.

The power of this model of product thinking is that we can apply it up and down the organizational hierarchy. Each team is driven by a clear vision for the change they are working to create. In organizations that are iteration-led instead of vision-driven, I've found that different teams in the organization are often iterating quickly but not always in sync.

Lean and Agile have taught us to harness the power of iteration through tight feedback loops—these execution methodologies give you speed. Radical Product Thinking gives you direction, helping you plan where you want to go and how you're going to get there. Combining iterative execution with Radical Product Thinking gives you velocity: speed with direction. The design firm PebbleRoad uses the illustration in figure 1 to represent the challenge it sees in organizations and the value of Radical Product Thinking.

This new mindset helps you take a more disciplined and visionary approach. The example of Singapore shows the importance of a clear vision that drives a strategy, priorities, and execution. Singapore didn't have many chances to iterate—it had seen other countries fall into decades of civil war by making mistakes in translating vision into execution. For many companies that build mission-critical products, iteration is not an option.

Iteration is helpful, but our iterations must be driven by a vision. We measure progress toward the vision to decide how to improve our next iteration. By taking this vision-driven approach, we engineer successful products to bring about the change we want to see in the world. Visionaries such as Lee Kuan Yew and Steve Jobs knew intuitively how to turn their concepts into reality. The rest of us could use a guide.

This book offers a clear, repeatable methodology for creating a vision-driven impact—from envisioning a change in the world to delivering it. It's a step-by-step approach to help you translate your

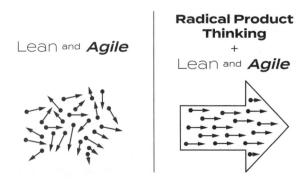

FIGURE 1: Lean and Agile give you speed, RPT gives you direction, the combination gives you velocity

vision so it permeates the daily activities that engage you and your team. Equally importantly, it's a shared language that makes communication easier and helps you bring others on the journey with you.

To introduce this new way of thinking, you need to start by understanding what gets in the way of building good products and the pattern of diseases that kill innovation. This vocabulary will help you spread this thinking within your organization—you'll be able to help others recognize these diseases so you can start to overcome or prevent them.

KEY TAKEAWAYS

- An iteration-led approach can move financial KPI up and to the right, but it doesn't guarantee that you'll build game-changing products.
- In an iteration-led model, iteration defines where you go. In a vision-driven approach, iteration helps you refine how you get to your destination.
- Radical Product Thinking helps you build vision-driven products that help you create the change you envision.
- Here are the three pillars of the RPT philosophy:
  1. Think of your product as your mechanism for creating change.
  2. Envision the change you want to bring to the world before engineering your product.
  3. Create change by connecting your vision to your day-to-day activities.
- Radical Product Thinking gives you direction, Lean and Agile give you speed. Together you get speed plus direction (i.e., velocity).
- In the RPT way, anything can be your product if it is your constantly improving mechanism to create the change you want to bring about.

CHAPTER 2

PRODUCT DISEASES

When Good Products Go Bad

Without a clear vision and strategy behind iterations, products become bloated, fragmented, directionless, and driven by irrelevant metrics. They catch what I now call *product diseases*.

Most of us learn to build products through trial and error and develop an intuition for building products. Using intuition to keep your vision connected to your strategy, priorities, and tactical activities is like doing algebra in your head. It works well for easy problems, but for more complex problems you can easily make a mistake. Products become diseased when the vision becomes disconnected from the execution. This happens often, which is why product diseases are ubiquitous across industries and sizes of companies.

Diagnosing a disease is the first step to curing or preventing it. The vocabulary around product diseases was designed to be memorable so that as you self-diagnose diseases, you'll be able to help others in your organization recognize them and buy into the need for a new way of thinking.

DISEASE 1: HERO SYNDROME

Hero Syndrome strikes when you focus exclusively on the *scale* of your impact at the expense of creating the change that genuinely inspires you.

Because of the business model of venture capital (VC) pushing companies toward higher-risk, higher-return decisions, VC-funded companies are especially susceptible to this disease. Here's the story of my own brush with Hero Syndrome early in my career.

The first company I cofounded, Lobby7, began as a VC-funded company. From the moment we raised funding, we were encouraged to "go big" and scale. Our sales efforts targeted companies with recognizable logos, our offices were in the financial district in Boston so we would seem big to our clients, and we were burning more money than we should have.

That was 20 years ago, but Hero Syndrome is still rampant,[1] and several very public failures have been caused by leaders focusing on the scale of their impact rather than on the impact itself. Cofounder and CEO of Beepi, Ale Resnik, raised $147.7 million to build a marketplace for buying and selling used cars. The management team was focused on creating a big impact and scale. As a result, their priorities were fundraising and valuation, followed by a great exit, rather than actually solving a problem for their customers. For example, customers would often get pulled over for having expired temporary license plates because the company didn't have its operations sorted out— getting titles and license plates to customers in a timely manner was an ongoing problem. The fundraising side, however, was looking better—Resnik told the *Wall Street Journal* in 2015 that the company was looking to raise a "monster round" of $300 million at a $2 billion valuation to fuel its national expansion.[2] Resnik was focused on the scale and public perception of his impact rather than its content; going big didn't result in a better product. While the idea of Beepi was great, the company was sold for its parts in 2017 when it failed on execution.

Hero Syndrome is especially alluring because some "heroes" do actually succeed in changing the world in highly visible ways and command a large share of media attention. In the business world, the giants may make the most noise, but small businesses are the engine of the economy.[3] Small businesses make up nearly half of private sector employment, and in the aftermath of the Great Recession, they led job creation, accounting for 67 percent of net new jobs created.[4]

When we let ourselves be consumed by Hero Syndrome, we end up focusing on the *need* to do something "big"—*need* implies coercion. Be kind to yourself and make the change that you *want* to see instead.

DISEASE 2: STRATEGIC SWELLING

Who hasn't suffered from the fear of missing out (FOMO)? It's easy to say yes to one idea or request after another, until you can't quite remember what you set out to do in the first place. Through this process, our potential for impact gets diluted. We spread ourselves thin across many areas and don't achieve any one goal at a breakthrough level. We call this Strategic Swelling.

By the late '90s Yahoo's home page was packed with features it had accumulated over the years—flashing pictures, horoscopes, financial news, groups, and much more. The company didn't want to miss out on any feature that a consumer could even remotely desire. The problem, however, was that most consumers had a measly internet connection at the time and the packed home page took ages to load. Google focused on just one offering: search. With its minimalistic home page, Google was infinitely faster to load and quickly overtook Yahoo as the dominant search engine because of Yahoo's Strategic Swelling.

Yahoo continued to expand its offering with a gluttonous appetite for acquisitions—it had caught an acute form of the disease. Here are a few of the 53 companies bought under CEO Marissa Mayer:

- Aviate (a smart home screen app)
- Polyvore (a Pinterest-like social commerce site)
- Tumblr (a blogging community)
- Skyphrase (a natural language processing startup)

At some point, so many features were packed on Yahoo's portal that you had to click on "More" to get an alphabetized list of all its offerings. When you need to alphabetize your offerings, you have a serious case of Strategic Swelling.

Prayag Bansal, a student in my innovation class at Northeastern University, insightfully summarized his learnings on Strategic Swelling at the end of a group project:

> As we defined our strategy, our product went from having many capabilities to having only one, well-defined capability. This was an eye-opener for me as sometimes *doing more does not necessarily provide better results*. Moreover, trying to provide a wide array of capabilities also leads to competing on more fronts and makes it harder to clarify your offering against the competition's.

A scarcity of resources can sometimes help you achieve more by preventing Strategic Swelling. When Bruce McCarthy was vice president of product at NetProspex, he saw an imminent danger from Strategic Swelling when the executive team gave him a list of 75 initiatives that they wanted his team to work on. But McCarthy had a small team of six people and got agreement among the executives to focus on just three initiatives that year. Over the course of two years the team launched a series of products, but each was deliberately related to the company's core product. By doing less, the team achieved more. They doubled their revenue each year and eventually sold the company to Dun & Bradstreet.

To recover from Strategic Swelling, organizations need a clear purpose that translates into priorities.

DISEASE 3: OBSESSIVE
SALES DISORDER

Obsessive Sales Disorder was first diagnosed in the corporate world. Anyone involved with quarterly revenue goals will recognize these fateful words: "The customer is ready to buy. They just need us to add one small feature to our product."

It's a tempting proposition that sounds mostly harmless. I remember uttering these words myself. But by the end of the quarter, while the sales team is popping the champagne over their thick stack of contracts, the poor engineering team has a road map a mile long that's completely driven by one-off customer requests rather than by the long-term strategic goals of the company.

Making this trade-off occasionally is one thing. But when we frequently give up long-term benefits to satisfy short-term demands, we're likely to be suffering from Obsessive Sales Disorder.

Looking beyond the business world, Obsessive Sales Disorder manifests in politics too. The phenomenon of global populism represents politicians trading off long-term thinking for short-term voter satisfaction. Take the populist agenda of curbing immigration as an example. Without immigration, the working-age population in the United States is projected to decline by 2035. With boomers retiring, the country needs foreign immigration to balance this decline in the working population and keep funding Social Security and Medicare.[5]

Funding the system is a long-term problem. An election, on the other hand, is a more immediate concern for a politician. So, while we have clear data on the need for immigration, politicians suffering from Obsessive Sales Disorder will make promises to restrict immigration, trading off the future in exchange for votes today.[6]

This is not to say that you shouldn't try to satisfy your constituents or that such a trade-off is always unacceptable. Such a stance would not be practical—you can't always work toward the long term without thinking about what needs to get done in the short term. In politics, it would limit what you can get done because you could never get reelected. In business, when you run out of cash, you lose your potential for impact. In fact, you quickly stop being a business at all.

Trading off progress toward a long-term goal occasionally so you can survive the short term is not unreasonable. But if you do it too frequently and you feel like you're losing your way, then you might be suffering from Obsessive Sales Disorder.

DISEASE 4: HYPERMETRICEMIA

Should a button on your website be red or blue? Test both options and see which one gets more clicks! While measurement is a powerful tool that can help us make better decisions, overreliance on measuring everything—rather than measuring just what you should—can lead to the dreaded disease of Hypermetricemia.

Hypermetricemia means focusing on "measurable" outcomes to determine success without sufficiently understanding whether these are even the right ones to measure to help you achieve your impact.

In the world of startups, vanity metrics such as venture capital investment raised, growth rate, or even the number of media mentions can become misleading indicators of the state of the business. Business has its typical "customer engagement" metrics: who wouldn't want customers to spend more time on your website more often? But if your goal is to help your customers finish a task and get on with their lives, maximizing time-on-site is taking you away from that goal rather than toward it.

To know what to measure, you need to understand what you're actually trying to achieve. When we choose to measure everything, we may end up measuring everything—except what really matters. Here's an example where that happened.

I was working for a company where we had a few hardware components that were failing. The company decided that to track what was going wrong and whether we were making progress in reducing failures, we would have video monitoring of all these components 24/7.

Six months later, however, we were no closer to knowing whether our efforts were reducing the number of failures. The videos were taking up so much data storage that we were keeping only one to two weeks of video feed and purging the rest! As a result, we could review hardware failures this week, but we didn't have videos from six months ago for comparison to tell if we were successfully reducing hardware failures.

In trying to measure everything, we didn't take a strategic approach to measurement to get the one metric we needed—a time series of logs from specific components that we should have designed the system to capture.

To overcome or prevent Hypermetricemia, we needed to derive the metrics we were measuring from a clear understanding of what we were trying to achieve (a vision and strategy).

DISEASE 5: LOCKED-IN SYNDROME

Locked-In Syndrome strikes when we commit to a technique, technology, or approach just because we have related expertise or because it has worked in the past. This can prevent us from exploring alternative solutions that might work better to achieve the impact we're hoping for.

When leaders at a large, successful company suffer from Locked-In Syndrome, it is commonly known as the Innovator's Dilemma. Since leaders are unable or unwilling to disrupt their own successful product lines, the company finds itself unable to compete as new technologies enter the market.[7]

In the '70s, IBM's dominance in the computer industry, with its industry-standard mainframes and hardware components, led to Locked-In Syndrome, which blinded it to the vast opportunity in software.

At the time, Commodore, RadioShack, and Apple had released personal computers (PCs), and every month IBM was falling further behind in an exploding consumer market. John Opel, IBM's CEO at the time, wanted to see IBM release a PC within a year. To achieve this goal, instead of building the components in-house, from scratch, the team decided to use off-the-shelf hardware components.[8]

To build the operating system, IBM engaged a software startup that was very willing to agree to all of IBM's requirements and the aggressive timelines. Under Opel's watch, IBM signed a nonexclusive license for the DOS operating system with the startup, now known as Microsoft.[9]

IBM was so locked in to the hardware business, executives failed to recognize the opportunity to become a leader in the software business as well. Ultimately, IBM's PC division was sold off to Lenovo in 2009, while Microsoft's profit margins ballooned over the following decades.

Getting locked in means forgetting about the actual problem you're trying to solve and instead focusing too much on your particular solution or approach. When you shift your focus to the problem, it becomes easier to recognize that there's more than one way to address a challenge, and it won't always be what worked in the past.

DISEASE 6: PIVOTITIS

A common refrain in the tech startup world is once things start getting tough, declare a pivot and take your company in a different (but related) direction. This face-saving maneuver allows companies to avoid problems rather than having to push through them. However, it often results in wild swings in product offerings and customer segments and leads to exhausted, confused, and demoralized teams—all sure signs of Pivotitis.

I experienced Pivotitis firsthand at a startup where I headed up marketing. We started out as a payment platform. Our vision was to be the next Visa, and we were tackling a really hard problem of acquiring both merchants and consumers. So we pivoted—we became a loyalty platform for merchants. But we soon realized that it was a crowded market, so we pivoted to a credit solution for small businesses. After some time I didn't know who we were and what we were asking anyone to sign up for on our website.

Like other diseases, Pivotitis is often justified by the cases where everything seemed to work out just fine. Business communication tool

Slack, for example, started off as a gaming company and then jumped into team chat, a completely different product and market. Keep in mind, though: when it entered the chat space, Slack shed all its baggage and preconceptions about being a gaming company. While this move is often called a pivot, the founder was really starting a new company.

If you lose confidence in the desirability of the change you envision, or if you decide it is simply unachievable, this should be a major decision that is acknowledged with adequate gravity. It would mean redefining your vision, strategy, and action plan. Recognizing this as a reset and a fresh start has a healthy side effect: it's no longer so easy to pivot wildly when things get hard or the next shiny object looks more attractive. It encourages you to push through challenges until they are proven to be truly insurmountable.

When we are inspired by the change we're working toward and driven by a clear vision, pushing through becomes more manageable. This helps us avoid Pivotitis, and keeps us from losing our way as we take detour after detour in pursuit of an easy path to success.

DISEASE 7: NARCISSUS COMPLEX

Narcissus Complex happens when we're looking inward and thinking about what we need to such an extent that we forget about the change we're trying to bring to the world. For example, when Boeing was focusing on its financial goals and conceived the MCAS to manage the 737 MAX's aerodynamic instability, that was Narcissus Complex.

A similar inward focus on company goals rather than on the customer was evident in early 2020 at the beginning of the SARS-CoV-2 pandemic. When some doctors and nurses wanted to wear masks in hospital elevators and hallways, some hospital administrators strongly discouraged the practice. They feared that healthcare workers wearing masks around the hospital would scare patients who might think that the hospital had a COVID problem.[10] When we look inward, we measure ourselves only by our results and the benefit to us instead of the impact on the customer.

This is not a call to be altruistic, but if we lose focus on the customer's needs, we focus on the local maxima and open up opportunities for competitors to find the global maximum.

COMORBIDITY

Most likely, you've recognized or experienced a few of the diseases in this chapter. It turns out that comorbidity is common with product diseases. In fact, the Berlin Brandenburg Airport (BER), which earned the nickname "ghost airport," has caught all seven of them.

After the Berlin Wall fell in 1989, the German government authorized plans for the Berlin Brandenburg Airport to mark Berlin's status as the icon of the reunification of Germany. BER was conceived as a world-class airport that would help restore Berlin as a global destination. Instead, it has become a monumental failure.

It was originally scheduled to open in 2011, but nine years later, it finally opened in October 2020. There were over 550,000 reasons for the delay—this is roughly the number of faults and failures that needed to be fixed before BER could open to the public.

What went wrong? I interviewed Martin Delius, who was a member of Parliament and the chairman of the inquiry committee. Delius read my article about product diseases and had already begun to diagnose BER when I interviewed him.

In diagnosing Hero Syndrome, Delius shared, "BER's vision was filled with superlatives." When the BER project started, agreement was reached on the broad vision: to build the most modern airport to mark Berlin as a global destination. I often see similar high-level agreement in organizations after teams spend a full day in an off-site meeting to craft a vision. Yet too often organizations come up with a fuzzy vision statement like "to be the leader in data storage and backup." The vision for BER was similarly vague, not detailed or actionable enough to uncover important misalignments.

These misalignments led to Pivotitis, repeated changes to the design after construction had begun. For example, the architect who drew the initial plans had a strong dislike for shopping, so he designed the airport without any duty-free shops. For the developer, this was a fatal flaw because a large percentage of airport revenues come from the stores. As a result, an additional floor dedicated to retail was added to the design.

BER had also caught Narcissus Complex—instead of focusing on market needs, the project focused on internal needs. BER was designed as a hub, which added to the project's expenses, even when all the airlines had said that they didn't want a new hub and didn't plan on switching.

Delius also recognized Strategic Swelling at BER: "Because the vision for BER was packed with superlatives, stakeholders including politicians in the federal government and the city of Berlin felt justified in adding on to the project to make BER bigger and better. In catering to these wishes, the project began to swell further." Delius came from a software development background and drew parallels from his experience of Strategic Swelling in software: "Often in companies with Strategic Swelling, features are all deemed 'high-priority.' Without a disciplined approach to prioritizing features, engineering teams are pressured to work harder and deliver more features. This happened at BER too."

Having caught Hypermetricemia, the team running the project often saw success as getting the contractor to absorb the cost of many of the changes. This in turn led to Obsessive Sales Disorder and trading off the long-term vision for short-term gains. "For example, a major contractor went bankrupt under pressure to deliver all the additional features requested without any additional resources." The pressure on the contractor may have produced short-term gains, but ultimately the bankruptcy led to further delays.

Lastly, BER had also caught Locked-In Syndrome—at some point it became painfully evident that demolishing the already constructed portions and starting afresh would be cheaper than pushing forward. But politicians were locked into the project and felt that they needed to show the public something for the money that had been spent. When BER eventually opened almost a decade late, it was more than $4 billion over budget.

Without a clear and actionable vision and strategy at the start of the construction, BER iterated its way from idea to implementation and caught every product disease along the way.

These seven diseases are the most common ones that you're likely to recognize in your organization—I've found symptoms of them in most industries. But this list is by no means exhaustive. You might be experiencing a disease in your organization that's unique to your industry and getting in the way of creating your impact. Calling a disease by name is the first step toward a cure.

Talk to your colleagues or have a group discussion about the diseases you're seeing in your organization. You can then begin to address each disease's root cause—either the lack of a clear vision and strategy or a break in the chain when translating the vision into action.

Part II of the book will help you avoid or cure these diseases—you'll learn how to craft a clear purpose through a vision statement and systematically translate it into your daily activities through your strategy and priorities.

KEY TAKEAWAYS

- These seven diseases are common across industries and sizes of organizations:
    1. *Hero Syndrome* strikes when we focus on external recognition instead of creating the change that inspires us.
    2. *Strategic Swelling* means building a wide range of capabilities but lacking the focus to develop any individual capability to a breakthrough level.
    3. *Obsessive Sales Disorder* means borrowing against the long-term vision to close short-term deals.

4. *Hypermetricemia* is focusing excessively on measurable outcomes to determine success, irrespective of whether those are the right things to measure.

5. *Locked-In Syndrome* means overly committing to a specific technology or approach because it has been successful in the past.

6. *Pivotitis* means changing direction whenever things get tough and leads to exhausted, confused, and demoralized teams.

7. *Narcissus Complex* means focusing on your own goals and needs to such an extent that you lose focus on the change you're trying to bring about.

- These diseases can be cured by starting with a clear vision and systematically translating it into your everyday activities.

PART II

THE FIVE ELEMENTS OF RADICAL PRODUCT THINKING

CHAPTER 3

VISION

Envisioning Change

Your product is your mechanism to create the change you envision for your users. This means that before you can build your product, you need to define your vision for the change you want to bring about. In this chapter we'll explore the humble origins of Lijjat to learn how to craft a compelling vision that drives you and your team.

Ever tried pappadums at an Indian restaurant? They're thin lentil crisps, often served with chutney. If you've had pappadums, most likely you've tasted Lijjat's products. Lijjat is the most renowned brand for pappadums with over 60 percent of the market share—the other 40 percent is fragmented among a large number of brands.

But on March 15, 1959, when the seven founders of Lijjat gathered on the terrace of a building to roll their first batch of pappadums, they weren't thinking about market share. They started with a modest vision but one that was deeply meaningful to them. They wanted to earn a dignified living and educate their kids, but being semiliterate, they couldn't expect to find jobs that would give them a reliable source of income.

They considered cooking to be their only marketable skill and decided to use this skill to address a market need that they observed. Consumers wanted pappadums that tasted like they were homemade. Growing up, I remember eating pappadums made by my grand-mother—a simple dinner of rice and dhal was transformed by the crunch of her fire-roasted pappadums on the side. But making pappa-dums at home was a labor of love and required skills well beyond those used in everyday cooking. This was the market need that the Lijjat founders could address with their cooking skills.

They borrowed 80 rupees (roughly the buying power of $150 today) from a mentor and social worker, Chaganbapa, and bought the necessary ingredients and the basic infrastructure to make pappadums. The seven founders made a pact that they would be equal partners and never take charity. They would share equally in the profit or loss, what-ever the outcome might be.

They sold their first batch of 80 pappadums to a local shopkeeper and came away with an order for more batches the next day. Within 15 days they had repaid their seed capital. Within 3 months 25 women were rolling pappadums and sharing in the profits. After 3 years the group had grown to over 300 women, and they no longer fit on the terrace. Women took home dough, rolled pappadums at home, and got paid when they brought back the rolled pappadums.

The founders remained committed to their vision of giving women the opportunity to make a dignified living by creating high-quality products that met consumer needs. True to this vision, they continued to add new members as equal partners. They were not building Lijjat with the goal of striking it rich.

Today, Lijjat has revenues of over $220 million and employs over 45,000 women. Its products have expanded from pappadums to spices, detergent, and soap. After 60 years, the founders are no longer roll-ing pappadums. But Swati Paradkar, Lijjat's president, described in an email interview how Lijjat's vision remains unchanged. The institution is still structured as a cooperative where all women are equal partners, referring to one another as sisters. They get paid for the number of pappadums they roll every day and share equally in the profit or loss every six months. They've never taken donations—in fact, Lijjat has made donations after major disasters, such as an earthquake.

Your vision aligns you and your team on the change you want to bring to the world. Your product is your mechanism to create that change—it's not the end goal in itself. To bring about this mindset shift, you need a detailed vision that is centered on the people for whom you want to create a better world.

Conventional wisdom says that a vision must be aspirational and big enough. Ideally, it should be captured in a slogan so it's easy to convey. But Lijjat's vision defies all of these common practices and has lasted well beyond the founders' tenure at the institution. What are the characteristics of a vision that finds its way into the hearts and minds of employees rather than the filing cabinet?

THE CHARACTERISTICS OF A GOOD VISION

Drawing from research through my work with a large number of organizations and teams on vision statements, I've found that a good vision has three important traits:

- It is centered on the problem you want to see solved in the world.
- It is a tangible end state you can visualize.
- It is meaningful to you and the people you intend to impact.

Center Your Vision on the Problem You Want to Solve

Vision statements often declare the management team's aspirations, such as "To be a billion-dollar company," "To be number one in our industry," or "To deliver shareholder value." Sometimes those aspirations are about revolutionizing, disrupting, or reinventing an industry.

Your vision shouldn't be about your aspirations for your organization at all. Instead, your vision should be centered on the change you want to create in the world, your impact. One sign of a good vision is that even if you were to take yourself and your organization out of the picture, you would still want the problem to be solved. If your vision is about your business goals, you're less focused on solving the customer's problem and are creating an opportunity for a competitor with a clearer focus on the customer's problem to beat you at your game.

When your vision articulates the problem clearly, your team can more easily understand the problem intuitively, and everyone has a clear purpose in solving it.

Visualize the End State You Want to Bring About

When you're creating change, you're creating something that doesn't exist today. To do this, you and your team must be able to clearly picture that world in your mind—you must have a shared vision of the world you want to create together. When your goal is a tangible, visualizable end state instead of something abstract, people can internalize it and make it their own dream. To create such a shared picture, your vision must be detailed—a short slogan fails to paint such a clear picture of the world that you want to bring about.

A descriptive vision helps you recognize when you're getting closer to your vision or straying from it. Your picture of the end state serves as a guidepost for you and your team to help you decide if you're on the right path to creating the world that you intended or if course corrections are necessary.

Galvanize Both Your Team and Your Customers

Often the sole focus of a vision statement is to create internal alignment. In reality, however, while your vision acts as a guide for your team, it will also form the foundation of your external messaging. Your vision must resonate with the people whose lives you want to impact, since you want them alongside you on this journey.

When you share your vision with your customers for the change you want to bring about for them, they should be nodding along with you. This is why you should steer away from vision statements like "To be a leader in our industry"—your customers don't care who the leader is! They just care that they have a product that solves their problem.

How do you know if your current vision meets these criteria? You can ask team members and some of your customers to share what they think your vision is. If your vision is clear on the problem you're setting out to solve and it resonates with them, they'll be able to state your vision in their own words—that's the true sign of a shared vision. If it doesn't resonate with them and they haven't internalized it, they may repeat back your slogan or feel embarrassed that they don't remember the vision statement.

Before you begin working on a vision statement, a word of caution. Studies have repeatedly shown that people are more motivated when they're solving a problem that's bigger than them—so it's tempting to write a vision statement that sounds righteous, even if you're solving a different problem.[1] But you must resist this temptation; be authentic.

In our conversation, Anne Griffin shared her experience as lead product manager at a blockchain startup: "We said that our vision was to make justice more accessible to people. But in reality, our customers were mostly law firms and we were continuing to build features to grow that customer base. So the vision wasn't really making justice accessible to people."

What Griffin describes is a symptom of Hero Syndrome, a product disease that happens when we try to concoct a vision that sounds bigger or more inspiring. Your impact doesn't have to sound big and it doesn't have to change the world for everyone. Your vision should be authentic so your team clearly understands the problem you're setting out to solve.

CRAFTING YOUR VISION STATEMENT

Even when you know the characteristics of a good vision, it's counter-productive to start with a blank sheet of paper.

Ever been at an off-site where you felt like you've played an exhausting game of Vision Bingo and came out with a vision that sounded much like what you had already? Starting with an empty sheet of paper creates pressure to find the perfect words that merit contaminating the pristine white. As a result, you tend to use the words you may have heard in the past to describe your vision, and the exercise often devolves into "wordsmithing" your existing vision.

To alleviate that problem and to make it easier for you to iterate on a vision without getting attached to the words, you can use the Radical Vision Statement written in a Mad Libs format:

Today, when [*identified group*] want to [*desirable outcome*], they have to [*current solution*]. This is unacceptable because [*shortcomings of current solutions*]. We envision a world where [*shortcomings resolved*]. We are bringing this world about through [*basic technology/approach*].

Below is this vision statement filled out for Lijjat:

Today, when [*underprivileged women from poor households*] want to [*run the household and educate their kids*], they have to [*depend on their husband's income, borrow from relatives, or take charity*]. This is unacceptable because [*in a patriarchal society they have little influence on household spending, and without a sustainable source of income their children's educational prospects are limited, thus repeating the cycle of poverty*]. We envision a world where [*women gain self-employment and thereby become self-reliant, leading to their socioeconomic progress*]. We are bringing this world about through [*manufacturing high-quality, fast-moving consumer goods that meet consumer needs without ever taking charity*].

Such a vision statement is radical and goes against everything you've learned traditionally about writing vision statements.

Whenever I do this exercise with teams, invariably the first question is, "Shouldn't a vision statement sound short and memorable? This sounds more like an essay than a statement!" Conventional wisdom suggests that you should have a short vision statement so it's easy for everyone to remember. Until now, the emphasis has been on *remembering* vision statements. Instead, the RPT way emphasizes *internalizing* the vision. It creates alignment and clarity on profound questions so that all team members can describe the vision in their own words.

I've found that common advice on vision statements has created a confusion between brand taglines and visions. A detailed vision makes the end state clear to your team so your vision is actionable and your team can use it to build the product. You can think of this fill-in-the-blanks statement as the blueprint for your construction team. The blueprint may have too much detail for a passerby to understand what you're building. So your marketing team uses the blueprint to craft a 3D rendering (brand positioning, image, and tagline, for example) to communicate to the world about what you do.

But even when you have a pithy version and images that you use for external communication, as a member of the construction team, you need the blueprint to be able to build the product. You'll find that having this detailed vision is handy when you are in a heated discussion or at a decision point. You'll be able to refer to it and ask, "Are we being true to this vision?"

Your vision must be detailed enough that it is able to exclude certain actions—that is, not all actions or activities should be compatible with your vision. This too is a radical departure from the conventional wisdom that your vision should be broad and aspirational. You should be able to test your vision by looking at different opportunities and scenarios and asking, "Is this aligned with my vision?" If every opportunity fits your vision, your vision is too broad and you need to add more details to articulate the Mad Libs statement.

Even if your end goal is utterly audacious, your near-term goal should be more achievable. You can use the Mad Libs statement above for your near-term vision and the following vision evolution statement to help you lay out the end goal:

> We started by changing the way that [*customer segment*] did [*activity/ outcome*] through [*basic technology/approach*].
>
> We've learned and grown since then, and now believe that the next big step is [*end state*].

SpaceX started by building a reusable rocket—its near-term goal was theoretically achievable and could be laid out in a road map. Its vision evolution, on the other hand, would be the audacious goal of enabling human life on Mars.

WHAT YOUR VISION STATEMENT MUST ANSWER

The Radical Vision Statement is designed to align teams on the *who, what, why, when,* and *how.* To craft your vision using the Mad Libs statement, you may find it helpful to think through the following questions:

- Whose world are you trying to change? Who are the people who have the problem you're inspired to solve?
- What does their world look like today? What are they trying to accomplish and how are they doing it today?
- Why is the status quo unacceptable? (Keep in mind that maybe it's not.)
- When will you know that you've achieved your vision?
- How will you bring about this change?

Let's explore how you can answer each of these questions.

Whose World Are You Trying to Change?

The *who* question helps you identify the group of people you intend to impact. Your answer should be as specific as possible. For example, it cannot be as broad as "consumers" or "businesses." It must be a group distinguishable from others so you can identify their problem specifically.

In Lijjat's case, the organization doesn't try to change the world for all women but specifically addresses the needs of women who are not educated and want to earn a dignified living.

When answering whose world you're setting out to change, list all the possible groups whose lives you're impacting and prioritize them. For example, Amazon's e-commerce business serves two segments: consumers who want to buy goods and merchants who want to sell their wares. Amazon takes a clear stance in prioritizing the customer segment over merchants—in the case of a dispute, for example, it takes the consumer's side.

Your answer to "Whose world are you trying to change?" has far-reaching consequences in terms of the outcome and even the business that you build. For example, had Lijjat's vision prioritized consumers' needs over giving women a way to earn a dignified living, it would have been a valid vision but one that led to a very different end result. Lijjat today measures success by the number of women who become financially independent as a result of working at the institution. If Lijjat's vision had prioritized consumers, it might have measured success by its market share and consumer satisfaction with its product.

This is not to say that Lijjat's market share or consumer satisfaction is unimportant. Of course, if Lijjat didn't produce good pappadums and its revenues tanked, it wouldn't achieve its goal of maximizing the number of women who can become self-reliant.

What Does Their World Look Like Today?

Put yourself in the shoes of the people you want to help and ask, "What is the problem they face today? What are they trying to accomplish and how are they going about it today?"

Most of the Lijjat sisters came from poor families and their educational prospects had been limited as kids—most were young when they had to drop out of school to contribute to the household income. As a result, their job prospects were grim as adults.

Paradkar, who was elected president of Lijjat in 2009, started her journey at the institution at the age of 10 when her father passed away and her mother became a member of Lijjat. Together with their mother, Paradkar and her three sisters rolled 65 to 75 pounds of pappadums every day to make ends meet.

She herself became a member in 1971 and continued her schooling while rolling pappadums on the side. Through her work at Lijjat, she was able to educate her two sons, who now have families of their own and live comfortably. Such stories are echoed by other women who joined the institution.

The problem that Lijjat founders wanted to address was that in a patriarchal society, unless they could bring in their own income, they couldn't influence household spending and direct spending toward educating their children.

Why Is the Status Quo Unacceptable?

The next question gets to the *why* of your vision. You've articulated the problem, but why is it imperative that it be solved? What are the consequences if it's not solved?

In Lijjat's case, the answer to why the status quo was unacceptable was very clear: Without the financial independence to educate their children, many of these families would have continued to perpetuate the cycle of poverty.

In writing your vision, you have to be open to the possibility that perhaps the status quo doesn't need changing. We have come to look at disruption as inevitable and always leading to progress. "Disrupt or be disrupted," venture capitalist Josh Linker proclaimed in his book *The Road to Reinvention*.[2] The *Harvard Business Review* article "The Innovator's DNA" quotes former CEO of eBay Meg Whitman as saying that innovators "get a kick out of screwing up the status quo. They can't bear it. So they spend a tremendous amount of time thinking about how to change the world. And as they brainstorm, they like to ask: 'If we did this, what would happen?'"[3] But screwing up the status quo without a clear picture of the end goal often leads to an iteration-led approach. When we're vision-driven, we don't disrupt for the sake of disrupting—we ask, "Is the status quo unacceptable?"

In asking this question, it's important to recognize that while you may see the status quo as unacceptable, the people you intend to impact may not. Take the example of the Segway. It was launched with fanfare in 2001 on ABC's *Good Morning America* as a better alternative to walking to work. Most customers, however, didn't walk to work, and few felt like their urban walking commute was unacceptable. The lesson from Segway is that your vision may be meaningful to you, but it must also be meaningful to the people you want to impact.

When Will You Know That You've Achieved Your Vision?

The *when* question should describe a visualizable end state and what success looks like.

It's tempting to write a high-level description of the end state. For example, Lijjat's desired end state could have been described as "Empowering women"—it's easy to remember and a catchy enough tagline. But it fails to describe how the organization would achieve this vision and leaves many unanswered questions. In what way would the women be empowered? How would the Lijjat sisters recognize that they have succeeded in empowering women? In answering these questions, you create signposts so you know if you're making progress or if you need to course correct.

For Lijjat, the desired end state is to create a world where women from low socioeconomic status households can earn a sustainable living, have more of a voice in household spending, educate their children, and lift the next generation out of poverty.

How Will You Bring about This Change?

In answering the *how* question, you can finally talk about the product, technology, or approach that helps you to bring about the change you envision.

Lijjat's mechanism for bringing about change is high-quality products for consumers that can be produced by the member sisters at home. Lijjat started with pappadums and has since expanded into other packaged goods, products including spices and soaps.

By describing the mechanism for bringing about your desired change, you make your vision actionable for the team. As you execute on your vision, you may discover that your mechanism needs refinement—in fact, this is why RPT defines *product* as a constantly improvable mechanism for bringing about the change you desire.

SPREADING YOUR VISION

To make sure that your vision gets translated into tactical activities, you need your vision to spread across your team and organization. Lijjat built its reputation to be synonymous with quality, even though its 45,000 member sisters manufacture products at home. The opportunity for discrepancies in quality is enormous. For Lijjat to deliver on the promise of high quality, the vision had to be deeply internalized by the 45,000 member sisters.

The RPT vision statement was deliberately created in a Mad Lib format to help you create similar buy-in. You can use it in a group exercise to craft a vision as a team—this format helps you stay focused on the content rather than the wording. In my workshops I've found that even in a two-person startup, founders most likely have different answers to the *who, what, why, when,* and *how* questions. It's important to air the differences so you can create a shared vision.

To do this in a group exercise, write the fill-in-the-blanks vision statement on a whiteboard and have each person answer the *who, what, why, when,* and *how* questions on sticky notes and place the notes in the blanks. You can then go around the room and share your answers and discuss similarities and differences with the goal of crafting a version that you agree on as a team. In a facilitated session, writing such a vision takes only one to two hours—but the time it saves in the long term by aligning the team on the details is immeasurable.

It's important to note that keeping buy-in and alignment requires revisiting your vision statement periodically. The questions of *who*, *what*, *why*, *when*, and *how* are existential questions and your answers may change. You may find that the landscape has shifted, and the answer to "What does their world look like today?" may have changed. The COVID-19 pandemic is a prime example of a market shift—the problem that you had set out to solve may have changed subtly or in more significant ways. You may also have learned more through your execution, so your answers to the *who*, *what*, *why*, *when*, and *how* questions may have changed.

You'll want to review your vision statement as a group regularly. In a more mature market, your cadence might be once in six months. In an immature market or a startup, you may find it helpful to review your vision once a month if you're discovering new things about the market or if it's evolving quickly.

Crafting and reviewing your Radical Vision Statement as a group ensures that each person on the team can participate in this vision. But beyond participation, internalizing the vision requires developing a deep sense of responsibility for the change you're creating—you need every person on the team to experience the status quo you want to change.

At Lijjat, the member sisters come from poor households and have experienced the inability to earn a dignified living. As a result, they have a sense of shared responsibility for changing the lives of other women in the same situation. Producing high-quality pappadums is their mechanism to deliver on their vision, and as a result they are visibly committed to quality control. Paradkar explains, "At every stage of production, member sisters are so conscious about maintaining high standards and the right quality that it is nearly impossible for any nonstandard piece of pappadum to go undetected."

Every Lijjat sister experiences the impact of the organization's vision in creating a better future for her family—this is an important factor in internalizing the vision. If the impact of your vision isn't as easily visible, you may need to create opportunities for team members to experience it.

When Danny Lewin cofounded Akamai, a content delivery network and cloud services provider, he had a big vision. But in the process of building Akamai, instead of imposing his vision on the team, he gave people the chance to experience the power of that vision so they would internalize it. Andy Ellis, chief security officer at Akamai, shared with me in a 2019 interview how Lewin spread his vision by creating what Ellis calls "visionary moments."

Lewin and Ellis built Akamai's first secure content delivery network (CDN) designed for financial transactions in late 2000. But when they started working on it, they hadn't quite figured out how to make the product secure in a way that would be satisfactory to financial services customers. At the time Ellis was the lead architect for the product. "I'll be honest. Danny had a huge vision and even though I was building it, *I* didn't really believe in it," Ellis recalls.

The turning point for Ellis came early one morning when Lewin asked him to explain to the leaders of a well-known financial services firm why they should trust Akamai's secure network. Ellis recalls, "I was barely awake and wondered myself why in the world they should trust it. At the time, the dot-com bubble had burst, we were hemorrhaging money and hemorrhaging customers. It wasn't looking good."

But Ellis got on the phone and described the product to the customers and how it would help them. "When I was done, there was silence . . . and then I heard one person whisper to his colleague, 'That's better than we would have done.'" Ellis describes it as his "visionary moment." The moment he saw the impact of the vision on the customer was when he went from being the person who was asked to help realize someone else's vision to the person who owned that vision.

Lewin died less than a year later in the 9/11 attacks—he was the first casualty of that day. But his legacy lives on at Akamai, Ellis says. "I try to give other people what Danny gave me: the visionary moment when they can see the impact of the vision. Because then *they* are going to drive the vision."

Ellis shares, "This mindset has helped us build a massive company carrying between 15 to 30 percent of web traffic, successful beyond what any of us would have predicted 18 years ago."

One technique you can use to create visionary moments is to get team members to observe users struggling with the status quo. To accomplish this at scale, Atlassian, a company that builds products for software developers and project managers, often produces a video to illustrate a team's vision. Sherif Mansour, distinguished product manager at Atlassian, explained in our conversation, "The video shows users struggling with the problem we're setting out to solve and the solution we envision for our users. It always has a voice-over that describes the same in words so everyone has the same interpretation of the visual." You can create visionary moments across the company by helping individuals see users' problem firsthand and how your solution can make their lives better.

In addition to creating visionary moments, it's important to help all individuals see how their role contributes to the vision. Translating Lijjat's collective vision into what it requires from each member sister is key to the success of its operating model. For example, Lijjat's vision of giving women self-employment means that the 45,000 member sisters are all equal owners of the institution who share in the profits equally. As a thought experiment, imagine 45,000 equal partners in a law firm or a consultancy who are asked to share profits equally, regardless of their seniority and how much they're billing. Unfathomable, right? And yet this model has worked at Lijjat for over 60 years. This equal distribution of profits requires individuals to think differently about compensation, in a way that aligns with the vision.

Lijjat's pledge is its instrument for translating the collective vision into what it means for each individual. Paradkar explains, "Each sister becomes a member and co-owner of the institution by signing the institution's pledge form." The pledge details the responsibilities the member sisters agree to. For example, they commit to rolling at least five kilos of pappadums per day. But it also describes the mindset member sisters must adopt for profit sharing: "No one in a family counts the number of pancakes one eats when they sit together for dinner. Similarly, I shall also not put that type of calculation while sharing [profits]. Instead of thinking in terms of 'I should get more than others', I shall aspire that others should not get less than me."

Every member sister has a clear sense of the collective vision and how she contributes to it through her behavior and role, whether it's through kneading the dough, distributing the dough, rolling pappadums, or collecting the rolled pappadums. The concept of communicating how every role contributes to the shared vision is equally applicable in the corporate world. We may have leaders with a clear vision, but all team members, whether software engineers or customer service representatives, are using their roles to create the collective change the organization seeks.

To spread your vision across organizational boundaries, you can encourage every team to build a vision for how the team can contribute to the collective vision through their work. Some Radical Product Thinkers even choose to write a vision statement as an individual to articulate the impact they want to have through their work.

Whether or not you choose to go to that level of granularity, as a manager, you can talk to all individuals on the team on how their role contributes toward the team vision. You may find that people with similar skills could have very different ideas for the impact they want to create through their work.

To build vision-driven products, we need to have a clear vision for the world we want to bring about. A good vision must act like a signpost so we know if we're making progress or if we need to course correct. It sets the direction so that the success of our iterative execution is not measured merely by moving financial KPI up and to the right but by whether we're bringing about the world we set out to in the first place.

KEY TAKEAWAYS

- Crafting a compelling vision is the first step to envisioning the change you want to bring to the world.
- A good vision is
  - Centered on the problem you want to see solved in the world.

- o A tangible end state you can visualize.
- o Meaningful to you and the people you intend to impact.
- You can craft a good vision using the Radical Vision Statement in the Mad Libs format to avoid getting distracted with wordsmithing and focus the effort in a group exercise on answering the following hard questions that will help you uncover and resolve misalignments:
  - o Whose world are you trying to change?
  - o What does their world look like today?
  - o Why is that status quo world unacceptable?
  - o When will you know that you've achieved your vision?
  - o How will you bring about this change?
- Once you have a clear vision, it's time to spread your vision:
  - o Get buy-in from the team by cocreating your vision using the Radical Vision Statement template.
  - o Help your team internalize the vision by observing users' frustrations with the status quo and seeing how your solution will make users' lives better.
  - o Cultivate visionaries by empowering every team in your organization to craft a vision statement that aligns with the organization's vision. Show individuals how their work contributes toward the team's and organization's vision.

CHAPTER 4

STRATEGY

Connecting the
Why with the *How*

Now that you've clearly articulated your vision, you need a product strategy to identify how you'll achieve this vision. The story of microcredit illustrates the importance of connecting your vision to your product strategy.

In 2006, economist Muhammad Yunus and Grameen Bank shared the Nobel Peace Prize for pioneering microcredit with the vision that it would eliminate poverty. But as microcredit was commercialized beyond Grameen Bank, studies in recent years show mixed results. Not only was the take-up of microcredit lower than expected, but even for those who took the loans, the effects weren't transformative in alleviating poverty. What went wrong? The vision around eliminating poverty was clear and purposeful, but it turned out that issuing microcredit wasn't the right strategy for bringing about that change.

The fundamental assumption behind microcredit as the solution to poverty was that most poor people were entrepreneurs at heart. Yunus believed that the pain point for the majority was that they lacked the small amount of capital they needed and that if they just had access to credit, they could start small businesses.

Anecdotal case studies illustrated how a $20 loan, for example, allowed a woman to start a small business making cane baskets and expand into making cane furniture. It seemed that by rolling out microcredit on a large scale, we could lift entire communities out of poverty.

Thirteen years later, 2019 Nobel laureates in economics Esther Duflo and Abhijit Banerjee pioneered a scientific approach to economics. In their book *Poor Economics*, they argue that anti-poverty policy has often failed over the years because of an inadequate understanding of poverty. Their studies showed that in the case of microcredit, some of the core assumptions around poverty were flawed.[1]

In planning microcredit as the strategy to address poverty, the assumption that most poor people are entrepreneurs was a generalization. Microcredit could address the needs of the entrepreneurially inclined, but it was never going to be the solution to all poverty. The assumption that access to credit was the pain point for most poor people was flawed.

The second major assumption about microcredit was that by investing in their business, borrowers could increase their income levels. However, just as some startups succeed while others don't, not all borrowers saw returns from investing the microloan into their business. On average, the effect of microcredit wasn't transformative.

Further, as any founder would attest, being an entrepreneur is all-consuming. Duflo and Banerjee's research indicated that those who invested their microcredit into their business were spending more time on it. So even when the business was going well, the borrower no longer had the time to work a second job. The end result was that on average, their net income remained roughly the same.

Instead of being a solution to poverty, microcredit started to become a problem when it was commercialized beyond Grameen Bank. Many social entrepreneurs saw microcredit as an opportunity to build personal wealth while alleviating poverty. For example,

Compartamos Banco, a Mexican bank, went public in 2007, and SKS Microfinance in India raised $358 million in an initial public offering.

These institutions focused on optimizing for financial metrics, and the vision behind microcredit became disconnected from the strategy and execution. When Grameen bank offered microcredit, the organization invested in educating borrowers on financial literacy and the effects of compound interest. In contrast, companies commercializing microcredit focused on aggressive marketing and debt collection.[2] Without financial literacy, borrowers didn't understand the implications of compound interest and often took on more debt to repay existing loans. While companies viewed loan repayment as a measure of success, in reality, many borrowers were stuck in a cycle of increasing debt.

The final nail in the coffin for microcredit came when the companies commercializing microcredit increased interest rates to increase profits. This move effectively changed the business model of microcredit, putting it in direct conflict with the goals of the people it was supposed to help. A higher interest rate also led to a thriving loan-shark industry. It eroded trust with borrowers who felt like the companies were taking advantage of them and stopped paying back their loans, taking the microcredit industry to the verge of collapse.[3] Yunus, who once saw microcredit as the solution to poverty, sharply criticized how the model evolved to essentially profiteering from poverty.

The example of microcredit illustrates that even when driven by a radical vision, a product can go awry in the absence of a cohesive strategy.

In the RPT way, product strategy means asking the following four questions with the mnemonic RDCL (pronounced "radical"):

1. *Real pain points:* What's the pain that triggers someone to use your offering? In the case of microcredit, the assumed pain point was that most poor people were entrepreneurs who needed access to capital to start or grow a business.
2. *Design:* What functionality in your offering solves that pain? Microcredit was designed as the solution for the pain point

above so entrepreneurs could lift themselves out of poverty. Duflo and Banerjee showed that while microcredit was helpful for some entrepreneurs, it wasn't the right design for solving poverty. Their scientific approach to understanding the problem of poverty showed that real pain points and design cannot be based on assumptions alone—they must be validated in reality.

3. *Capabilities:* What capabilities or infrastructure do you need to deliver on the promise of the solution? For microcredit to work, Grameen Bank invested in financial literacy for borrowers. Companies commercializing microcredit invested in a different capability: aggressive marketing and debt collection. Their capability wasn't aligned with the design or the real pain points and microcredit took a turn for the worse.

4. *Logistics:* How do you deliver the solution to your users? Aligning a sustainable business model with the real pain points, design, and capabilities was important to Grameen Bank, so it charged low interest rates and kept costs low by having staff live in dorms. Companies commercializing microcredit raised interest rates, and the logistics of the business model became disconnected from the vision and strategy.

When our real pain points, design, capabilities, and logistics aren't aligned with the vision, it can spell doom for our product, like it did for microcredit.

HOW TO CRAFT YOUR OWN RDCL STRATEGY

A good product strategy must comprehensively address RDCL and be grounded in reality by testing any assumptions. You can use the RDCL strategy canvas in figure 2 and follow these four steps to document your own. This canvas is also in the Radical Product Tool Kit, which you can download from RadicalProduct.com.

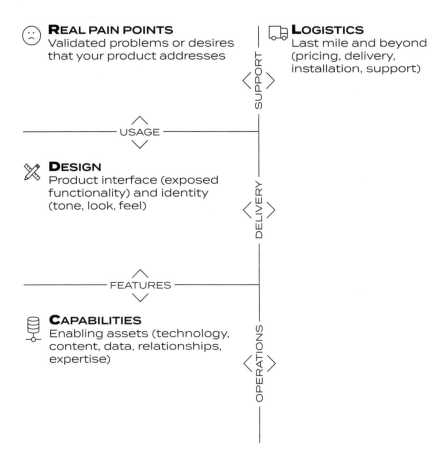

FIGURE 2: RDCL strategy canvas

Step 1: Discover Users' Real Pain Points

To create the change you envision through your product, people must engage with your product. This, in turn, requires a deep understanding of who needs to interact with it and what pain points they are trying to solve when they turn to it.

Looking back at the case study of Lijjat, we see that the organization has given financial independence to 45,000 women because the founders deeply understood the social conditions of the women they wanted to empower—they understood the real pain points.

To arrive at real pain points you need to identify who will use your product and understand the pain that makes them engage with your product. What are they trying to achieve?

The founders of Lijjat never intended to empower all women. They were specifically addressing the needs of women in low-income households who wanted to earn a living but whose job prospects were grim because they lacked education. Most of these women lived in a profoundly entrenched patriarchy that required them to be mainly at home and be caregivers for children and elderly parents living with them. They could take a job only if the family approved of it, which in turn would be possible only if the women were able to work from home and meet their caregiving obligations. Lijjat was able to change the lives of so many women because its operational model was based on a deep understanding of these real pain points.

How can you apply these lessons in defining your target if your customers are other businesses? Describe your target customers and their pain in detail. For example, in my conversation with Jana Gombitova, product manager at Akvo, a not-for-profit technology and data tools company, she could have described her target market as IT leaders. Instead, as a Radical Product Thinker she described her target market as "IT leaders in governments and NGOs [nongovernmental organizations], most often in remote areas, who want to get better at data-driven decision-making but don't have in-house expertise in data analytics."

It's tempting to define your market broadly. But products that try to do everything for everyone risk working for no one. Founders often worry that being too specific about their target customer segments will limit their potential market size. This worry is understandable—it's important to think of your future expansion trajectory. However, if you can't drive initial adoption in a small population of well-targeted customers, that future you're preparing for will be moot anyway.

In defining your target customers and their pain points, it's important to verify that a pain point is real. The RDCL acronym is conveniently pronounced "radical," but Nidhi Aggarwal, Geordie

Kaytes, and I chose R for "real pain points" (instead of P for "pain points") very deliberately. To be real, pain points must be validated. Microcredit went wrong because the pain points pursued were not validated. If you do not validate the pain points, the rest of your strategy is built on a shaky foundation.

To be validated, a pain point must be both valued and verified. Here's an easy-to-remember formula:

Validated = Valued + Verified

For a pain point to be valued, your user must be willing to give up something in exchange for having the problem solved. This exchange can be in the form of a fee to use a product that solves the problem. But even in the example of free products such as social media, the user is giving up privacy and time in exchange for using them.

If the pain point is not valued, monetizing your product becomes hard. In the startup ecosystem, the common refrain goes "First get traction, then think about monetization." The inherent risk with this approach and ignoring whether users value a pain point is illustrated by the following example.

Medium, a blogging platform founded in 2012, raised $132 million in venture funding over a period of eight years. Yet it was never clear who would pay for content on the site. The platform's initial growth was fueled by quality content created by writers who were paid from Medium's war chest of funding. However, as it became clear that this wasn't a sustainable strategy, the company made several failed attempts at an ad-based business model before finally settling on charging users a subscription fee of $5 per month. However, Medium had never validated that users valued its "well-researched explainers, insightful perspectives, and useful knowledge with a longer shelf life" enough to pay for it.[4] A Nieman Lab article in 2019 described the first seven years of Medium as "countless pivots" and "an endless thought experiment into what publishing on the internet could look like." In other words, Pivotitis.[5] In 2020, Medium was still not profitable.

In addition to being valued, to be real, a pain point must also be verified. Have you observed that others feel this pain, or do you assume that customers have this need? This verification is especially important if you've felt the pain personally—scratching your own itch can be a powerful vision motivator, but you have to confirm that others share that itch too!

Jeremy Kriegel, a UX designer I've had the opportunity to work with on several occasions, shared with me his experience at a medical startup. The founder was a doctor and was sure that the solution he had developed for note-taking was exactly what doctors wanted. After all, he himself was a doctor and he would have used it. Only after observing other doctors did he realize that his pain point wasn't the same as others'. Kriegel shared his lesson from this: "To verify that the pain point is real, you must start with a crack of doubt and the feeling that maybe, just maybe, you're wrong about what your user needs." This crack of doubt is the basis for your research.

Esther Duflo and Abhijit Banerjee found that governments and NGOs are often so sure about their assumptions on poverty that they forget to test these assumptions scientifically. Microfinance fell into this same trap. The techniques and best practices for interviewing and observing users are out of the scope of this book, but you can look to *Interviewing Users* by Steve Portigal and *Just Enough Research* by Erika Hall for practical tips and techniques for user research.

Once you've identified the target customer segments and their validated pain points, you can begin to prioritize them. In developing a new product, especially a radically innovative one, chasing multiple customer needs across different customer segments will drain your resources and slow your progress toward achieving your vision. It's unlikely that you could address all pain points at once: by acknowledging this and prioritizing pain points, you're giving your team an actionable strategy.

Step 2: Design Your Radical Product

Design helps you solve your users' pain by answering these questions: "What are they interacting with to solve their pain?" and "How do they feel when they interact with your product?"

Ever since Steve Jobs gave us the delightful phrase "Design is how it works," design has played an increasingly big role in product strategy. However, beyond some basic principles, it's difficult to say what constitutes a "good" design for your product.[6] It's easy to evaluate design in hindsight: were your customers able to use your product easily and did it make them happy? However, these questions don't necessarily do you any good when you're trying to figure out *how to design it in the first place.*

The Radical Product Thinking answer to "What is good design?" is relatively straightforward: a "good" design is one that fits into and advances your overall strategy. When we talk about how a product is "designed," we are talking about how we can intentionally shape how people use our product (the interface) and how they perceive it (the identity).

Interface design is how you expose your product's underlying capabilities to your users. When paired with an enabling capability (such as data, expertise, or algorithms), the details of an interface are often called features.

One feature of Lijjat's operational model is that women roll pappadums at home. If the women had had to work at a factory, they wouldn't have been able to meet their responsibilities as primary caregivers and their families would not have been supportive of their work. Without this feature, the organization would have engaged very few women.

Another key feature of the design is that women get paid every day for the pappadums they roll—this enables them to influence day-to-day household spending. By contributing to daily income and being able to influence daily spending, they develop confidence and have a voice in directing household income toward their children's education. These features reflect the deep understanding of the real pain points.

We've come to think about interfaces as the visual user interface for a product. But your user might interact with your product in several different ways. For example, if you go to your bank to deposit a check, the interfaces you experience include the physical interface of standing in line to wait for the teller, the human interface when you speak to the teller agent, and a paper interface in the form of the paper deposit slip that you fill out.

To discover all the interfaces for your product, start by understanding the motivations of your end users and what they're trying to get done. What features would support users in accomplishing their goals?

Do not get stuck in the tasks that users are doing today to get the job done. For example, if bank users' motivation is to deposit money in their accounts, a bank that is trying to optimize the status quo might make the waiting area more comfortable so users can have a seat while waiting for their turn. Instead, focusing on the motivation allows us to rethink the design. We must ask the question, "How do we support users in what they're trying to get done?" In this example, a bank could support tech-savvy users trying to deposit their checks by allowing them to accomplish this from the comfort of their homes through an app.

In addition to thinking about how users interact with the product, in designing a product we have to think about how users perceive the product and how it makes them feel.

The look and feel of a product are often treated as if they are unrelated to solving customers' actual problems. In fact, the visuals, voice, and overall feeling of the product can have a dramatic impact on your product's usability: UX researchers at Nielsen Norman Group have found that beautiful products are given higher usability ratings than they "deserve."[7]

Beyond aesthetics, matching your product's voice and tone to your customers' expectations is critical. This can greatly affect the desirability of your brand, impacting both buying decisions and day-to-day usage in the same way that visual design can.[8]

The importance of a product's design identity doesn't mean you should strive for form over function. It just means that for maximum impact, your product design should take into account the humanity—social, emotional, even irrational—of your users, prospects, and customers.

Lijjat's design identity takes into account how member sisters want to be perceived. Beyond earning a dignified living, member sisters want to feel self-reliant and valued as members of society. Lijjat has developed educational programs for member sisters, providing literacy and basic financial skills to them. These programs are designed to address their identity needs so that when women educate their kids, they themselves shouldn't feel left behind.

To work through the identity of your product, start by looking at the real pain points you have identified, and consider the following questions:

- What emotions are your users experiencing when they face these pain points?
- Given those emotions, how should using your product feel? Exciting? Relieving? Fun?
- What can you do with visuals, audio, text, or other experiential aspects to create these desired feelings?[9]

Defining the "right" design for your product's interface and identity is a strategic task. You should leave the actual designing up to expert designers, but if you provide them with the right strategic guidance, you are much more likely to end up with a marketable product that effectively solves your users' pain points.

Step 3: Define Your Capabilities

Defining the capabilities in your RDCL strategy means answering the question, "How will you deliver on the promise of your design?" You can think of your design as the body of your car—it's both form and function. The design includes the unique look and the curves of the exterior of your car. It also includes function—it's the number of doors your car has, the finish of the seats, and how much space you have in the back. Design determines how you interact with your car on an everyday basis. Capabilities are what lie under the exterior: they include the engine, the electronics, and all that powers your car.

If you've ever fundraised, most likely investors have wanted to know, "Why are you the right people to deliver this solution?" They're essentially asking you about capabilities. Capabilities are the special sauce you have (or need to develop) in your organization that powers your design.

Your capabilities can be tangible, such as data, technology, architecture, and infrastructure, or intangible, including relationships, partnerships, and processes.

An example of a tangible capability at Netflix is its viewership data, which powered the company's recommendation algorithms. Competitors didn't have a similar volume of viewership data to replicate the accuracy of Netflix's recommendations.

A tangible capability that was key to Netflix's success in its early years was the iconic red envelope it used to ship DVDs to customers. This simple envelope looks trivial, but it represents one of the earliest patent applications Netflix filed, and it powers the company's design of shipping DVDs to consumers and processing returns.[10]

The post office typically processes and stamps 40,000 standard size envelopes an hour in crushing metal drums—a DVD would be easily damaged by this violent treatment. Envelopes classified as "flat mail," however, are spared this treatment.

The patented red envelope is a tangible capability Netflix developed so its DVDs could be mailed at the price of one first-class envelope and be classified as flat mail.

Your design could also be powered by intangible capabilities such as trust or relationships. When Airbnb was started, its founders realized that to deliver on the promise of their design (a marketplace where anyone could offer or rent temporary accommodations), they needed both guests and hosts to trust the platform. Consumers are accustomed to seeing reviews before making a purchase. But when Airbnb was starting out, it had very few users and, as a result, very few reviews, which in turn made users hesitate to try it out.

To break this vicious cycle, Airbnb needed to invest in an intangible capability: getting consumers to trust the listings on the website by having someone from Airbnb visit the properties listed and take high-quality pictures to verify the claims in the listings. This wasn't sustainable in the long run but was part of a strategy to increase trust in the system until the review mechanism was self-sustaining.

Capabilities lie under the hood and power the design. When you're driving your car, you enjoy the feeling of the ride, the bass on your sound system, and the seat warmers on a cold night. But you rarely ever think about what's under the hood—except when your car doesn't turn on or starts coughing.

The design should abstract the capabilities so that users can enjoy their experience through the interface and how the product makes them feel rather than worrying about what's under the hood. Your users should experience only the design. But capabilities enable you to uniquely deliver on the power of your design.

Step 4: Define Your Logistics

Defining the logistics means answering questions about the customer experience surrounding product acquisition—that is, the path that your product takes to your customer. Our traditional definition of *product* as the hardware or software we deliver often leads us to overlook the logistics component of strategy. When *product* is defined as a physical or digital object, we focus narrowly on building the object— elements of the product experience such as installation, pricing, and support become afterthoughts.

If you were building a house, you'd think about pricing and maintenance as integral to the design. For example, for a family with kids, you wouldn't build a family room with white carpet. If you were developing a property to rent out, you'd pick different appliances than for a house you planned to live in. When you think of your product as a mechanism for creating change, your pricing plan, support, training, and maintenance become part of your comprehensive strategy and guide your decisions.

Here are some questions you could consider to define the logistics for your product:

- How does your product get into people's hands? Through what channels will you sell it?
- On which platform will they be using your product—for example, is it a paper-based form or an app on their mobile device or a web page that they'll primarily access from their desk?
- Will people need training in how to use your product? How will you support them if they have issues?
- What's your pricing and business model?

It's important that the logistics for your product are aligned with the real pain points for customers. Often companies try to layer on popular approaches to pricing or delivery that are favorable to them, even if they are not particularly well suited for the specific product or the customer. For example, the recurring revenues from a subscription pricing model make it tempting to impose subscriptions on every product. As a result, sometimes products that may be perfectly suited for one-time payment get unnecessary features tacked on to justify a recurring pricing model.

Juicero illustrated the danger of this approach. Consumers would typically expect a juicer to be a one-time purchase of a kitchen appliance. However, because a subscription model was more attractive to the company, Juicero's product wasn't designed to squeeze fruit. Instead, it slowly squeezed expensive juice pouches that the user had to purchase on a subscription basis. While this model was doomed for failure, the product died an accelerated death when a viral YouTube video illustrated that a person's hands could squeeze these pouches more efficiently than the Juicero "juicer."[11]

Logistics can, if used strategically, help differentiate your product from your competitors, and should be an important consideration from the inception and development of a product. Defining each logistics element with your sales and marketing teams upfront is a great way to align the product strategy with the go-to-market plan.

THE ROLE OF ITERATION

Instead of being iteration-led and finding local maxima by optimizing for financial metrics, a good RDCL strategy helps you stay vision-driven by anchoring your iterations around the real pain points your users face, your solution to these, and your business model to support it.

The abundance of credit during the economic boom of the 2010s led to an overreliance on iteration. We often had the luxury of trying what works without a comprehensive strategy that answered the four RDCL questions. But now that you understand the importance of a RDCL strategy, you see why it's hard to arrive at the right answer to each of the four questions through iterations alone.

You can iterate more efficiently by thinking through the RDCL questions and validating assumptions through observing and speaking with your users. In crafting your RDCL strategy, do not expect to get all the answers right the first time but rather to put a stake in the ground based on what you've researched. You'll then need to test your strategy against reality.

This is where iteration comes in. You can iteratively test and improve on the RDCL strategy you crafted. Through your execution and measurement, you'll test how well your design is working to address the real pain points. You'll refine the capabilities that help you deliver on the promise of the design and improve how you deliver the solution to your customers through logistics. Just remember to regularly review your RDCL strategy to update it based on the learnings from your iterations. Your RDCL strategy is the bridge between your vision and your tactical activities.

In the next chapter we'll learn how to prioritize tactical activities in a way that aligns with the vision for the change you want to bring about. It's an approach that you'll be able to use more broadly in your organization to balance progress toward the long-term vision against the reality of your everyday business needs.

KEY TAKEAWAYS

- Your product strategy is how you translate your vision into an actionable plan.
- A comprehensive product strategy answers the following four questions (an easy-to-remember mnemonic is RDCL, pronounced "radical"):
  1. *Real pain points:* What's the pain that triggers someone to use your product? Remember that the pain points are real only if you've validated them: Validated = Verified + Valued.
  2. *Design:* What functionality in your offering solves that pain? Design means thinking of the interface (how you want the product to be used) and the identity (how you want the product to be perceived).
  3. *Capabilities:* What capabilities or infrastructure do you need to deliver on the promise of the solution? Capabilities can be tangible (e.g., data, intellectual property, contracts, people) or intangible (e.g., relationships, skills, partnerships, trust).
  4. *Logistics:* How do you deliver the solution to your users? How do you price it and support it? Logistics is often an element of strategy that is bolted on as an afterthought. Your revenue and cost model, training, and support plan should be considerations in your product development plan.
- Once you've crafted a RDCL strategy, you can use iterations to test and refine your strategy.

CHAPTER 5

PRIORITIZATION

Bringing Balance
to the Force

To build vision-driven products, you've defined a clear vision and a strategy. Prioritization is how you can infuse your vision in your everyday decision-making.

In making everyday decisions, you're intuitively balancing your long-term goals against short-term needs. If you worked purely in pursuit of the long-term vision without acknowledging the reality of survival, you may not survive long enough to make progress toward your destination. On the other hand, in the absence of a clear long-term purpose, your short-term goals, typically profitability and business needs, would become the sole focus. Building vision-driven products requires balancing progress toward the vision while dealing with the practicality of survival.

You may have developed an intuition for finding this balance through your years of hard experiences and learning through trial and error. To use a *Star Wars* analogy, through years of experience you may have learned to use the Force. However, in the corporate world, as in the movie, it seems that a select few in the organization have the Force and others don't. Those who don't have this intuition find it harder to make their own decisions and try new things—they have to await guidance from those who have it. Organizations would be more effective if everyone had the Force and dictating the right trade-offs didn't fall to a few. It turns out that we all have the Force in us—we just need to learn to use it.

Cultivating this intuition in teams is not just a nice-to-have; it's crucial for building vision-driven products. All individuals are contributing to the vision and are making trade-offs between the long term and the short term through their own work. A software developer could choose to spend time carefully building software for the long term or could write code quickly to deliver something in the short term and undertake major repairs later. No leader could dictate all the trade-offs at every level. To build vision-driven products, you'll need to rely on every individual to make the right trade-offs.

You can scale your thinking across the organization by developing in others the same intuition you have for trade-offs. When you take this approach, you won't need to micromanage because you'll be influencing others to make decisions like you would, even when you're not around.

The RPT approach to alignment on prioritization and decision-making gives teams and individuals autonomy to make decisions. Research shows that companies that offer autonomy are 10 times more likely to outperform traditional organizations in the short term and more than 20 times more likely to outperform them in the long term.[1]

This chapter helps you achieve these benefits by using a powerful two-by-two framework. It will help you infuse your vision into your everyday decision-making and give teams a shared intuition for making the right trade-offs.

VISUALIZING THE TRADE-OFFS

When you use intuition to prioritize and make business decisions, you're essentially trading off between making progress toward your vision (vision fit) and mitigating short-term risk (survival). You can visualize balancing the two using the two-by-two rubric shown in figure 3.

In an ideal world, of course, everything you're working on will be a good vision fit and help you survive. Realistically, however, many aspects of your decisions and priorities will represent trade-offs between vision fit and survival. Here's how to think about the trade-offs represented by the four quadrants of the rubric:

- *Ideal quadrant:* Items in the top right quadrant are those that most closely match your vision and improve survival by mitigating risk. These are the easy decisions. But focusing only on opportunities in the Ideal quadrant would mean a persistent focus on the immediate benefits.
- *Investing in the Vision quadrant:* To progressively deliver on the long-term vision, you need to also selectively pick projects in the Investing in the Vision quadrant. These are typically

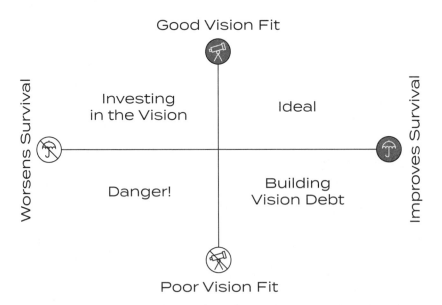

FIGURE 3: RPT prioritization rubric using vision fit versus survival

projects that will bring long-term benefits but increase risk in the short term.

- *Building Vision Debt quadrant:* Occasionally you may need to take on projects that reduce short-term risk but may be a poor fit for your vision; pursuing them results in vision debt. You have to take on vision debt very carefully, knowing that incurring too much will derail what your product stands for.

- *Danger! quadrant:* Items in the bottom left quadrant are a poor vision fit and expose you to additional risk. Pursue items in here only if they unlock important opportunities in the future.

Of these quadrants, decisions that fall in the Ideal and Danger! quadrants are the easiest. The harder decisions are in the Investing in the Vision and Building Vision Debt quadrants. If we want to build vision-driven products, our trade-offs should be more often in the Ideal and Investing in the Vision quadrants while avoiding Building Vision Debt and Danger! quadrants as much as possible.

MANAGING VISION DEBT

You incur vision debt when you put progress toward your product vision on hold to satisfy more immediate financial constraints. If you are in the tech industry, you may be familiar with its tech counterpart: technical debt. Accumulating tech debt leads to buggy software and brittle code, while accumulating an excess of Vision Debt leads to confused customers, demotivated teams, and a directionless product.

You're probably taking on vision debt whenever you do one or more of the following:

- Build unique, custom solutions for each customer
- Add one-off features and integrations to your product just to close a sale
- Use a competitor's technology, content, or data in the core of your product

- Build features that increase revenues but trade off user privacy and well-being

All of these activities represent opportunities to get to market faster, close deals, and increase revenues, but they move you further from achieving your vision. If you need the cash, however, taking on vision debt may be necessary. Just be sure to keep track of activities that incur vision debt, and make a plan with your team to pay it down later in your strategic road map.

But be careful. Like any debt, vision debt comes with compound interest. The longer your product has diverged from your core vision, the more difficult it will be to get executive and team buy-in to return to the central vision of your product.

Once you have chosen to incur vision debt, communicating this choice to your team is critical. Your team will quickly recognize that the product is moving away from the vision they've all been asked to buy into. Publicly recognize this fact, and describe the long-term strategic thinking behind it. By acknowledging vision debt, and explaining the plan to pay it back, you can mitigate any short-term damage to your team's alignment and commitment to the vision.

Nidhi Aggarwal, founder of QwikLABS and cocreator of the Radical Product Thinking framework, was able to successfully leverage vision debt to build up a sustainable customer base in her startup's early days. The product enabled students to easily access hands-on training labs to learn cloud computing configuration management. Two years after the launch, Aggarwal received a call from the company's biggest customer. It wanted QwikLABS to develop specific labs just for its own use (more of a consulting arrangement than a product purchase).

Becoming a professional services company was not aligned with the QwikLABS vision but would help short-term survival and growth. After much debate, the QwikLABS leadership team decided to take on the vision debt, directing several developers to focus exclusively on creating content and features for this single client. Normally, this would be an example of the product disease Obsessive Sales Disorder, but Aggarwal and her executives were explicit in acknowledging to the team that this represented a short-term step away from the vision. Most importantly, they committed to a timeline for getting back on track, ensuring that the team saw this as a temporary but necessary detour, not as a top-down loss of confidence in the vision.

INVESTING IN THE VISION

When you invest in the vision, you indicate to your team through your actions that you value the vision and that it affects your decision-making. To get your team to buy into the vision more deeply, you need to role model investing in the vision.

You're probably investing in the vision if you do the following:

- *Spend time fixing technical debt (the technical shortcuts you took when building the product that helped you get to market faster):* Addressing technical debt means you're not working toward delivering an additional feature in the short term, but in the long term it gives you a stronger technological foundation to continue adding features.
- *Spend resources on user research:* Investing resources to conduct research may not yield immediately visible results, but it helps you build a better product in the long term.
- *Invest in R&D:* This activity doesn't help your bottom line immediately, but unless you're investing in R&D, your lead will eventually be eroded.

All of these activities represent opportunities to make progress toward the vision, but they don't help your chances of survival in the short term. You'll need to evaluate how much you can afford to invest in the vision based on the magnitude of your survival risk.

DEFINING SURVIVAL

A radical vision provides clarity on the long term when using the vision-fit-versus-survival rubric as a communication tool. Similarly, you'll find that defining survival gives you a shared understanding of the biggest short-term risk that threatens your product. Making this definition explicit instead of relying on each person's intuitive notion of survival helps ensure that everyone is aligned with the end goal in a way that helps you survive long enough to achieve that goal.

Survival is about identifying and mitigating the biggest risks that could shut you down. Your risks will evolve over time but typically fit within the five categories shown in figure 4.

Technology or operational risk is the risk that you might not be able to invent key technology or solve operational issues (such as scalability) that are critical to your business model. Legal or regulatory risk might result in your company being sued or otherwise legally prevented from operating. Your top concern may be personnel risk if your product would not survive the departure of key personnel. If you're the founder of an early stage company, your biggest risk is usually running out of cash (financial risk). On the other hand, in a large company, even if your product is losing money, the company often has the ability to pull cash from its reserves or from other, more profitable operations to keep paying employees and suppliers. Your biggest risk may come from a powerful but skeptical stakeholder who wants to pull the plug on your product (stakeholder risk).

Technology or
Operational Risk

Legal or
Regulatory Risk

Financial Risk

Personnel Risk

Stakeholder Risk

FIGURE 4: Survival risk–the biggest risk that could kill your product tomorrow

While all of these risks are important, not all of them are going to get you simultaneously, but like a gazelle, you can effectively run from only one or two at a time.

You can define your biggest risk by writing a Survival Statement—a sentence or two that encompasses the gravest and most immediate dangers to your product's existence. This will work as the counterpart to your Radical Vision Statement.

The following fill-in-the-blanks statement makes it easy to craft a Survival Statement as a group exercise:

> Currently, the greatest risk to our product's existence is that [*greatest risk*].
>
> If this happens, we won't be able to continue operating because [*consequences of risk*].
>
> This risk will most likely come true if [*factors that increase or amplify risk*].
>
> Some factors that could help us mitigate this risk are [*factors that decrease/mitigate risk*].

EXAMPLES OF SURVIVAL STATEMENTS

For Likelii, a startup I founded in 2011 and sold in 2014, the risk that we couldn't show product-market fit (and would thus be unable to raise additional funding) represented financial risk. This is the Survival Statement I would have written for Likelii:

> Currently, the greatest risk to our product's existence is that [*we may not be able to raise venture funding*].
>
> If this happens, we won't be able to continue operating because [*we won't be able to make payroll*].
>
> This risk will most likely come true if [*we fail to demonstrate traction through user growth*].
>
> Some factors that could help us mitigate this risk are [*focusing on growing the user base over the next six months, giving us time to seek funding before our cash runs out*].

A Survival Statement for a larger company may look different. When I was working at a large enterprise, our customers were cable companies with sales cycles measured in years. Our product addressed a key pain point and was much simpler and faster to use than existing products in the market. It effectively replaced multiple tools and interfaces that the end users were juggling, and this drove rapid adoption.

When the company was acquired by a much larger company, the new parent company had a similar product in its lineup, although it wasn't nearly as easy to use (and in fact required a large support staff dedicated to helping customers with basic tasks). However, a large, politically powerful contingent within the parent company preferred the existing in-house solution.

This is the Survival Statement I would have written when I was heading up product management at that company:

> Currently, the greatest risk to our product's existence is that [*we lose executive sponsorship for our product*].
>
> If this happens, we won't be able to continue operating because [*our budget will be zeroed out and our team will be reassigned to other projects*].
>
> This risk will most likely come true if [*stakeholders don't value the importance of the simplicity and speed of our product, and we have not gathered political capital by driving sales into new accounts*].
>
> Some factors that could help us mitigate this risk are [*cultivating relationships with stakeholders at the acquiring company and getting their support while growing sales over the next year*].

To write a Survival Statement, start by identifying all of the risks you can name within each of the five risk categories (financial risk, stakeholder risk, personnel risk, legal or regulatory risk, and technology or operational risk). Then, depending on your scenario, pick one or two of these classes of risk that might be nipping at your toes more than the others.

Once you've identified your biggest risk, think about the biggest consequences of this risk. What would happen if the risk were to come true? If our early stage startup failed to raise funds, we would no longer be able to pay employees, and that would kill our product. In a larger company, if a skeptical stakeholder were to pull the plug, we'd no longer have the resources to continue working on the product. One trick to identify the consequences is to keep asking "So what?" until you arrive at the final consequence.

Next, think about how you would mitigate your biggest risk. At an early stage startup, you may be able to mitigate risk by showing specific financial metrics to convince your investors that you are a worthwhile investment. In a larger company, if your biggest risk is losing stakeholder support, evaluate what may cause you to lose that support and how you could prevent it.

PUTTING THE PRIORITIZATION RUBRIC INTO ACTION

Using the vision-fit-versus-survival rubric for prioritization helps simplify the discussion on priorities and can become an ongoing communication tool. The Avenue Concept (TAC), a nonprofit in public art, used the two-by-two rubric to communicate its three-year strategic plan to the board and to its own team.

The organization, and specifically the executive director, Yarrow Thorne, had accomplished a series of major installations of public art including sculptures and murals and was laying the groundwork for art infrastructure in the city of Providence, Rhode Island. Over time, as awareness grew of TAC's ability to complete public art installations in short periods of time, other organizations and even individuals began to reach out to the nonprofit to engage it on new projects.

TAC's team members began to feel stretched thin across too many projects and were wary of catching Strategic Swelling. They realized the need to carefully manage their resources to maximize impact. The team used the two-by-two rubric to prioritize their strategic initiatives and shared these with the board so that the organization could plan its budget and resources appropriately. TAC began by defining the two axes:

- *Vision:* TAC's vision was to create a deep social impact by bringing art into public awareness.
- *Survival:* For TAC, as for many nonprofits or startups, survival was defined as continued access to funding.

With these concepts defined, the TAC team evaluated and plotted opportunities into quadrants as shown in figure 5:

- *Ideal quadrant:* For TAC, the Sculpture and Mural Programs were close vision fits—they were both very visible and therefore raised awareness of public art. Because TAC's executive director had crafted a model that allowed the team to scalably source and install artworks, these programs fit in the Ideal quadrant. But focusing only on opportunities in the Ideal quadrant would have been myopic.

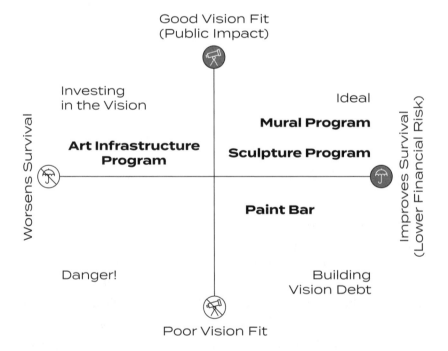

FIGURE 5: Prioritization rubric for The Avenue Concept

- *Investing in the Vision quadrant:* To progressively deliver on the long-term vision, TAC was also selectively investing in projects in the Investing in the Vision quadrant. TAC's Art Infrastructure Program installed lighting to highlight installations in the evenings. The lighting raised the visibility of the artworks in the dark and brought art into the evening ambiance—as a result, the program was high on the vision fit axis. But on the survival axis, developing this art infrastructure across the city was resource-intensive, so it presented a higher financial risk. TAC used the two-by-two framework to explain to the board that investing in the vision increased the organization's fundraising needs and required the team to pick selectively from this quadrant.
- *Building Vision Debt quadrant:* One way of offsetting some of the fundraising requirements was to thoughtfully take on vision debt. The Paint Bar (TAC's paint store and studio for local artists) was an example of using vision debt wisely to get to the next milestone. The Paint Bar didn't create deep and meaningful impact through art for the public, but it brought in revenues through paint sales. It made creating murals more sustainable for TAC and promoted engagement with local artists.
- *Danger! quadrant:* TAC didn't have opportunities in the Danger! quadrant.

TAC used this two-by-two framework to align its board and the team on its strategic plan and the rationale for the projects the team was selecting to deliver on the vision.

Similarly, at an executive level, you can evaluate your strategic initiatives and prioritize them based on the quadrants they fit in. You could also use these to discuss major sales opportunities and how they fit with the overall vision.

Product teams can use these to prioritize features. Start by drawing the two-by-two rubric on a whiteboard and restating your two axes (vision fit and survival). Write each feature on a sticky note and as a team decide which quadrant each feature belongs in.

Most likely you'll prioritize more features from the Ideal quadrant and a few from the Investing in the Vision quadrant. You'll want to avoid what's not a good vision fit as much as possible while being practical about survival. It's a balance. For example, Spiro.ai, the AI CRM (artificial intelligence customer relationship management) startup, dedicates 25 percent of engineering bandwidth to work on the Investing in the Vision quadrant in each sprint.

What's most important in this exercise is that all team members should be able to engage in this discussion and share their rationale for why a feature belongs in a particular quadrant. As individuals get comfortable sharing their rationale using the two-by-two rubric, it becomes a helpful tool for communicating your rationale for your priorities to stakeholders. This communication helps to continuously reinforce the alignment between product teams and executive leadership on the product vision.

Using the two-by-two rubric for prioritization is an easy way to bring Radical Product Thinking into your organization. Teams at any level—whether the executive leadership team or a product development team—can use it to infuse the vision into their everyday decision-making.

YOUR PRIORITIES (AND YOUR RUBRIC) MAY EVOLVE

Most likely, your rationale for priorities will change over time and you'll find that your vision-fit-versus-survival definitions may need to evolve. Just as your vision requires periodic review to account for changing market conditions, the same applies to survival. Your biggest risk might change over time, and your rubric for decision-making should change to accommodate this evolution. If your Radical Vision Statement needs to change, it's important to acknowledge that and communicate the new trade-offs. Every time you use the two-by-two rubric, start by restating your two axes and confirm they are still valid.

Explicitly stating your two axes is also helpful because your priorities aren't uniform across an organization. A team working on a long-term R&D project may write a Survival Statement focused on the technological risk, whereas a team working on an existing product may define survival by financial risk.

In larger companies with multiple products, each team's priorities are driven by that team's specific vision and the survival risk, which may be different from those of another team. Each team should write vision and survival statements and create its own two-by-two to balance the long term against the short term.

When you're talking to someone on a different team and draw up a two-by-two, you can pick which product's vision fit and survival you're referring to or you may choose to refer to the vision fit and survival axes at a company level if you're talking about your collective priorities. The prioritization rubric is a communication tool to explain your rationale for priorities and decision-making across the company.

SIMPLICITY OVER PRECISION

The Radical Product Thinking approach to prioritization is based on a clear choice of simplicity over precision. Many companies choose to create complex spreadsheets to calculate numerical rankings for priorities. The simple two-by-two rubric is deliberately, radically different. It's designed to develop intuition so that, like Jedis, everyone in the organization can learn to use the Force and find the right balance.

A few years ago, when I started consulting for a company to help increase alignment in the organization, product teams were using a numerical approach to prioritization and decision-making. The company culture was very analytical and data-driven and this desire for precision permeated the prioritization process. One product team showed me their painstaking work in prioritizing over 150 features: The team had picked five principles that were important for the product and scored each feature on how well it achieved a certain principle. Each of the principles had a weighting, and once the team had scored a feature against the five principles, the spreadsheet would spit out a magic number that indicated the feature's priority from 1 to 150. The spreadsheet looked really detailed and seemed very precise.

But it turned out that this approach was giving the team a false sense of precision; no one could explain why a particular feature ranked number 57. The rationale always came back to the spreadsheet itself: "Well, this is how the feature ranked on the five principles and hence its priority." While the team had a list of priorities, they didn't have an intuition for making the right trade-offs; the product leader's influence on decision-making was limited to the spreadsheet.

The magic spreadsheet approach to prioritization had another undesirable side effect: its complexity was leading to fewer prioritization discussions with stakeholders. These discussions, when they happened, often devolved into tweaking the scores and masked the more fundamental misalignments. When we switched to the RPT approach to prioritization, several leaders commented that it had become easier to understand the team's rationale for prioritization and provide feedback.

The RPT approach to prioritization opens conversations and leads to a more facilitative approach. As a result, not only does this approach lead to more buy-in for decisions, it also leads to rich discussions that create a shared intuition in the team for decision-making.

You could spread your influence and help others develop your intuition by having others observe your decision-making without the two-by-two, but this approach takes a long time. In my workshops I often explain this with the analogy of doing algebra. Imagine you're introducing smart students to algebra. When you show them the problem $x - 1 = 0$ and tell them the solution is $x = 1$, your students will quickly see the pattern for solving the next such problem using intuition.

But the more complex your problems and the more variables, the harder it is to see the pattern and develop intuition. When we dictate priorities top down, the obvious decisions will make intuitive sense to your team. But for the more complex scenarios, the decisions and priorities you hand down to your team may seem arbitrary. Some may see your pattern and keep up, but others may not. By using the two-by-two and explicitly discussing trade-offs, you build intuition faster in your teams and bring the whole team with you on the journey.

Your vision gives you the drive and the purpose on this journey; it's like having a powerful engine in a car. Prioritization is like the tires—it's where your vision meets the reality on the ground (your business needs). To build vision-driven products, you need both the power of a good vision and the ability to translate that into priorities. The RPT approach to prioritization and decision-making helps your team internalize and use your vision every day.

KEY TAKEAWAYS

- In the Radical Product Thinking way, the two-by-two prioritization rubric is a strategic tool to help you communicate your rationale for prioritization and decision-making. To get started, define your two axes: vision fit and survival.
- Survival is defined by the question, "What is the biggest risk that could kill your product tomorrow?"
- The two-by-two naturally creates a facilitative approach for decision-making where teams can evaluate trade-offs by placing initiatives, opportunities, tasks, or features into the four quadrants:
  o *Ideal quadrant:* Helps you make progress toward the vision and lowers risk
  o *Investing in the Vision quadrant:* Helps you make progress toward the vision but increases risk in the short term
  o *Building Vision Debt quadrant:* Helps you survive in the short term but takes you further away from achieving your vision
  o *Danger! quadrant:* Takes you away from your vision and increases risk

- Examples of how you can use this approach to prioritization and decision-making include the following:
    o Communicating your strategic plan and its rationale to your team and board
    o Structuring conversations to make difficult decisions
    o Sharing your intuition on product decisions or trade-offs

CHAPTER 6

EXECUTION AND MEASUREMENT
Taking Action (Finally!)

To build vision-driven products, we must ensure that our vision and strategy are closely tied to our everyday actions and how we measure success. The story of Nack illustrates how products can go awry when the vision becomes disconnected from tactics and how we can stay vision-driven using the RPT approach to execution and measurement.

I first met Nack's founder, Paul Haun, over coffee when he told me about his company with his characteristically infectious enthusiasm. Haun started Nack determined to spread kindness around him through "random acts of coffee." He was inspired by the tradition of "suspended coffee" that started in Italy, where you'd buy one coffee and pay for two—the second paid forward for someone who could use a random act of kindness.

Haun built Nack as a mobile app and iterated on features to consistently delight users. He had read case studies on how the iPhone was an iconic product because it delighted customers and read the book that explained how Zappos found success by delivering happiness. Armed with these lessons, Haun, like many entrepreneurs, was iterating with the goal of delighting customers.

His app allowed users to find suspended coffees around the city and also create "random acts of coffee" by paying for suspended coffees. Nack's users were using the app almost daily, recommending it to their friends and frequently inviting others to join. As a result, Nack had enviable usage metrics including Net Promoter Scores, time spent on the app, and number of daily users.

However, although these popular metrics were pointing up and to the right, Haun's enthusiasm turned to dismay when he shared how things were going. It turned out that Nack users were just delighted by the free coffees—they were logging in every day to search for free coffees and driving distances to claim them. They weren't, however, paying it forward or spreading kindness through the app. Despite delighting customers through his iterations, Haun's product wasn't creating the change he wanted to bring to the world.

Conventional wisdom is that to build successful products, you test your features in the market and iterate based on what customers want—you have to be "customer-driven." In reality, getting customer feedback is like asking for directions when you're in the car—it helps you navigate better. As the driver, however, you have to know your destination to be able to get directions. Nack's features were customer-led rather than customer-driven.

Nack's loudest customers were the ones who complained that there were no free coffees in their vicinity. In trying to continue to delight customers, Haun had spent over $1,500 of his own money to fund suspended coffees through Nack. Yet he was no closer to spreading random acts of kindness (except his own).

Haun needed to connect his execution and measurement to his vision. In shifting his mindset to a vision-driven approach, Haun defined his product vision as promoting kindness among coffee drinkers, and Nack was his mechanism for bringing about this change. To deliver on this vision, the strategy focused on teaching users to gift coffee as a way of showing kindness. In translating this to action, Haun rebuilt Nack with a new set of features: whenever users received free coffee, they would always receive two—one to consume and the second to gift.

Brands wanted to be part of this movement to promote kindness and offered to fund suspended coffees. Users learned to give coffees that were funded by brands, but the feature created a fundamental change in user behavior. Users found joy in giving, and soon 27 percent of the users who gifted coffees funded by brands were using Nack to buy someone a coffee using their own money!

Instead of delighting users because they *received* free coffee, the new Nack made users feel good because they were *sending* someone a coffee. By translating a clear vision and strategy into execution and measurement, Nack was delighting users with the goal of creating the change Haun had envisioned.

This chapter will give you practical tips and tools to translate your vision, strategy, and priorities into execution and measurement. It'll help you make the best of vision and iteration through a hypothesis-driven approach to execution.

HYPOTHESIS-DRIVEN EXECUTION AND MEASUREMENT

Your product is a constantly improving mechanism to create change. To decide what to improve, organizations emphasize the need to make data-driven decisions. A data-driven approach to building your product is great—but only if you're measuring the right things. *Data-driven* is often taken to mean that the business and product are driven by metrics. Unfortunately, too often the metrics used are simply those that are easy to measure (e.g., registered users as a proxy for usage) or popular to measure. When products are driven by the wrong metrics, they catch Hypermetricemia.

Your product may seem successful when you track popular metrics such as daily active users, how likely your users are to recommend your product (Net Promoter Scores), and revenues. But each of these popular metrics comes with assumptions that may not hold true for your business.

A vision-driven product is not justified in itself; because it's a mechanism to create the change you envision, it's successful only if it's bringing about that change. This is why in the RPT way, instead of measuring *popular* metrics, you have to measure what's *right* for your organization.

The template in figure 6 can help you work through your execution and measurement plan. The main goal of this template is to help you identify the connection between what you're testing and what you're measuring—your hypotheses. You can write a hypothesis as a fill-in-the-blanks statement:

If [*experiment*], then [*outcome*], because [*connection*].

The hypothesis derived from Nack's strategy of teaching users to gift coffees would be written as follows:

If [*we give users two coffees, one of which they must gift*], then [*they'll start using their own money to gift coffee*], because [*they'll learn to gift coffee and enjoy it*].

Once you have a hypothesis in place, you can measure key metrics to know if the outcome was what you expected and if your experiment (or strategy) is working. For Nack, the key metric that indicated progress toward the vision of spreading kindness was the percentage of users who were spending their own money on gifting coffee.

The activities column in the template helps you list the tasks needed to set up your experiment and test the hypotheses you've stated. At Nack, before we could test our hypothesis, we needed to partner with brands to fund coffees as part of their marketing campaigns. We also had to develop the features to enable users to receive and gift coffees.

When you use this template, you can think about what metrics would indicate progress toward your vision and strategy. When you

INITIATIVE: _____

RESPONSIBLE TEAM/INDIVIDUAL: _____

✎ KEY METRICS
What measurable
outcomes are we
seeking?

☑ ACTIVITIES TO SET UP
YOUR EXPERIMENT
What concrete actions
should we plan to take?

? HYPOTHESES
How and why do we think we can create those outcomes?

If . . . EXPERIMENT	Then . . . OUTCOME	Because . . . CONNECTION

FIGURE 6: Radical Product Thinking template for a hypothesis-driven approach to execution and measurement

think about your vision as a hypothesis, you can measure progress by asking, "What metrics would indicate whether we're bringing about the world we describe in this vision?"

Similarly, each element of your strategy represents what you *think* will work. Your experiments and metrics will validate that. For each element of your RDCL strategy, you'll want to test your approach through an experiment and track metrics that indicate whether your actionable plan is working. Remember to go back and update your RDCL strategy as you learn from your iterative execution and measurement.

Here's an example of how you can use the execution and measurement template. At Likelii, we wanted to help users find wines they were likely to like. One of the elements of our RDCL strategy was our design to understand users' taste preferences without scaring them off. Our hypothesis was this:

> If [*we ask users to name a wine they like*], then [*most users will answer the question*], because [*it takes little effort to enter the name of a wine and they can get personalized recommendations right away*].

To test this hypothesis, we tracked a key metric: the number of users who were answering this question. Unfortunately, it turned out that users often had a hard time recalling the name of a wine they had enjoyed—only 20 percent answered this question! Our strategy of asking them to name a wine to get their taste preferences wasn't working.

To improve our strategy we developed the following hypothesis:

> If [*we create a simpler quiz to understand users' taste preferences*], then [*users will complete the quiz*], because [*unlike our original approach of asking them about their favorite wine, the new quiz doesn't create cognitive load*].

To test the above hypothesis, our activities included crafting a short quiz with pictures to get their taste preferences. To understand how tannic they liked their wine, we asked them how they liked their tea or coffee: black, with milk, or with milk and sugar. To understand their preferences on acidity, we asked which fruits they liked in their fruit salad. We deduced their tastes from simple questions.

When we launched this quiz, we found that our simplified approach was working—over 70 percent of users completed this quiz! Our measurements and iterations were driven by our strategy.[1]

Writing a hypothesis for each feature or element of your RDCL strategy may seem tedious, but you'll find that this hypothesis-driven approach becomes a way of thinking. As you've seen in previous chapters, the goal with RPT is to create intuition. The above template is designed to give you practice in thinking more deeply about metrics. Once you've developed muscle memory, this technique will become second nature and will feel like intuition. You'll begin to formulate a hypothesis in your mind every time you add a feature to your product or start a new strategic initiative in your company.

USING RADICAL PRODUCT THINKING WITH ITERATION

The examples of hypothesis-driven execution in this chapter illustrate that Radical Product Thinking pairs well with feedback-driven execution methodologies such as Lean Startup and Agile.

A hypothesis-driven approach means starting with the mindset that your vision and strategy are hypotheses. Radical Product Thinking helps you define and communicate what you're building and why. Lean and Agile help you execute, learn, and iterate under uncertainty. As you learn from your hypothesis-driven execution, you'll go back and refine your strategy, and possibly your vision, based on these learnings, as illustrated in figure 7.

To avoid becoming iteration-led, you must ensure that your Lean and Agile activities are driven by your vision and strategy. For example, Lean Startup emphasizes launching a minimum viable product (MVP), a version of a product with just enough features to satisfy early customers and provide feedback for future product development. It's important to think about your RDCL strategy when planning your MVP.

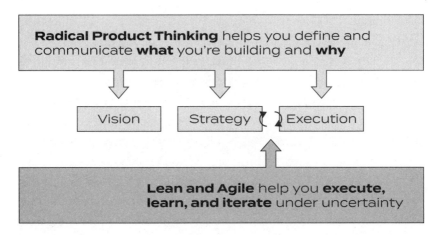

FIGURE 7: How Radical Product Thinking fits with Lean and Agile execution

Most likely you've heard the generalization that an MVP must be scrappy—often, it's followed by a quote from Reid Hoffman, founder of LinkedIn, saying, "If you are not embarrassed by the first version of your product, you've launched too late." This may be true for some markets, but it really depends on the RDCL strategy and the real pain points.

The key criterion for your MVP is that it must be *viable* as a solution to satisfy early customers. For example, at a robotics and warehouse automation company, the equipment was mission-critical to clients. If the system broke down, the customer's warehouse came to a standstill and lost money because of delays in outgoing deliveries. As a result, what was minimally viable to customers was a well-developed system with high uptimes and reliability. Compare this to a phone app for a shopping list—you could afford to start with a very frugal MVP. Your MVP should be derived from your strategy and meet the real pain points that are most important to your customer segment.

The nature of your MVP, in turn, will affect your strategy. For example, if you were building a warehouse automation solution like the one above, your startup would need to raise a large round of funding to deliver such a fully viable product as the initial offering.

You can also use RPT with your Agile development processes to build your product incrementally. If you're using Agile, sometimes the loudest customer decides what you're going to build next. This effectively leads to a "micropivot" every few weeks based on what features bubble to the top as most urgent. As the vision often becomes disconnected from day-to-day activities, your product is at risk of becoming a muddled mess of contradictory features and functionality.

You can avoid this risk by using the RPT approach for execution and measurement to communicate your hypothesis and the experiment you were running, what you learned, and how it's shaping the next set of experiments you're going to run. You can also use the RPT approach to prioritization as you plan what you'll build in your next increment—you can use the two-by-two vision-fit-versus-survival rubric to balance progress toward the vision and short-term business needs as you prioritize tasks and features.

As you learn from the experiments, you may discover the need to course correct or change your direction more dramatically. You could formalize this communication by setting up a regular cadence for reviewing your vision and RDCL strategy—for example, you may consider doing this every month as an early stage startup or every six months for a more mature product. Taking this approach helps you stay vision-driven as you continuously refine your product.

THE DANGER OF SETTING GOALS FOR PRODUCT METRICS

RPT defines a product as a continuously improving mechanism to create the change you intend. Once you know what metrics are important, you may be tempted to think that building a successful product is a matter of setting specific goals for your product metrics. After all, conventional wisdom says if you want to achieve something, you have to set measurable goals.

I often see product metrics used in setting Objectives and Key Results (OKRs), a framework used by many companies to define goals across the organization, assign responsibility, and track outcomes, for example, "Get over 20,000 new signups." In setting OKRs, teams are given the instruction to be aspirational and set ambitious goals.

Ironically, the goals that were designed to be aspirational become demotivating. Even high-performing individuals who are passionate about their product will advocate for less ambitious goal setting because of the fear of failing to achieve those goals.

In a joint paper titled "Goals Gone Wild: The Systematic Side Effects of Overprescribing Goal Setting," researchers from Eller College of Management, Harvard Business School, Kellogg School of Management, and the Wharton School recommend that "goal setting should be prescribed selectively, presented with a warning label, and closely monitored."[2] They found that although specific, challenging goals can produce positive results, these same characteristics of goals often cause them to degrade employee performance, shift focus away from important but nonspecified goals, harm interpersonal relationships, corrode organizational culture, and motivate risky and unethical behaviors.

When you are building products, setting goals for product metrics is particularly contraindicated. The process of building a product is filled with uncertainty where there are few right answers. Studies have found that on a complex task where a correct strategy wasn't obvious and when performance was more a function of strategy than of task effort, do-your-best instructions led to better results than specific goals.[3] In such cases, they found that specific goals may discourage experimentation and adaptive behavior and ultimately limit innovation.[4]

Another problem with setting goals for a few product metrics is that it narrows the focus to optimizing just those few metrics. To build successful products, you may have several hypotheses on what you could do better for your user, and as a result, you may be measuring and analyzing a large number of metrics. But OKRs are designed to get you to focus on just a few key metrics. Employees may optimize for those narrow measures of success, but this may come at the expense of other KPIs that you're not measuring. OKRs may be helping you reach the *local maximum* instead of the *global maximum*. In fact, researchers found that when individuals were given specific, challenging goals, it inhibited their learning from experience and degraded their performance compared to being given the simple instruction "do your best."[5]

The case against goal setting becomes even more damning when it comes to stretch goals. Studies have found that the use of goal setting for "management by objectives" creates a focus on ends rather than means. Researchers found that people who were given specific goals were more likely to engage in unethical behavior than people who were told to do their best. Even more importantly, they found that the relationship between goal setting and unethical behavior was particularly strong when people fell just short of reaching their goals.[6]

The example of Lucent Technologies' scandal in 2000 illustrates this adverse effect of stretch goals: the company reported that it had overstated its revenues by nearly $700 million. Richard McGinn, the former CEO of Lucent, was known for pushing audacious goals on his managers and had set the goal of achieving 20 percent annual revenue growth—an enormous target for a company with $30 billion in assets. Revenue magically appeared in each quarter, and Lucent committed $8 billion to "customer financing"—in essence, the company was giving away its product and labeling the transaction a sale.[7] In a complaint letter, a former Lucent employee charged that McGinn and the company had set unreachable goals that caused them to mislead the public.

We repeatedly see how goals lead to behavior that's not good for society. At Wells Fargo, executives developed a strategy of cross-selling products to their customers to increase their "share of wallet" with each customer. As part of this strategy, branch managers were assigned aggressive quotas for the number and types of products sold. If the branch did not hit its targets, the shortfall was added to the next day's goals. In 2016, the scandal broke that to meet these aggressive targets, employees had been opening new accounts without customers' knowledge—sometimes this even included forging signatures. In February 2020, Wells Fargo agreed to pay $3 billion in fines to settle the long-running probes into its fraudulent sales practices.[8]

Several studies have raised the possibility that people would resort to unethical behavior to reach goals, but these effects have been consistently ignored. Even in the seminal book on goal setting, authors Edwin Locke and Gary Latham predicted this effect, noting it as "the unintended dysfunctional effects" of goal setting. But they propose superficial solutions including creating "control systems" and firing employees who violate ethics to reach goals "regardless of any revenue streams they generate or costs they reduce."[9] Given that setting goals predictably leads to unethical behavior in both theoretical research and empirical studies, by continuing to use goals for management by objectives, we're ignoring evidence to perpetuate a system that damages performance and incites bad behavior while expecting different results.

Awareness of the perverse effects of goal setting is increasing, and some companies are modifying their approach. A minor step is divorcing OKRs from performance appraisals. In an article by Evan Schwartz, Laszlo Bock, senior vice president of people operations at Google from 2006 to 2016, explains why OKRs shouldn't be tied to performance: "Google tied OKRs for usage of a product directly to people's compensation. People started gaming the system to get their bonuses. The very idea of tying monetary incentives to hitting key results was thus deemed detrimental to both the product and the broader culture."[10] Bock and Google popularized OKRs, but to deal with the side effects, they recommend not using OKRs for performance management.

Unfortunately, divorcing OKRs from performance appraisals isn't enough—even when OKRs aren't tied to monetary incentives, the process of setting OKRs requires listing who is responsible for achieving a particular goal. This means if a goal is not achieved, everyone is aware of whose failure it was—it implicitly ties performance to achieving goals.

Another approach to deal with the side effects that Bruce McCarthy, author of *Product Roadmaps Relaunched*, recommends in his workshops on OKRs is to remember that OKRs can be recalibrated. If you see that the OKRs you set are the wrong indicators of progress or that they're impossible to achieve, you should change them.

Smaller companies may be able to recalibrate, but in larger companies OKRs are often coordinated across divisions—getting buy-in and setting OKRs every year takes incredible effort. If you discover during the year that some of the goals were set incorrectly, how much of the coordination and realignment are you willing to revisit? The prospect seems daunting. In fact, an executive in a large organization responded to the suggestion of readjusting OKRs periodically by saying, "We'd die if we had to do this many times a year." OKRs, once set, are hard to adjust, and teams may end up working toward a goal even when it's clear that it's not the right measure of success.

Indeed, this is what Spotify stated when it announced on its *HR Blog* that it's no longer using OKRs:

> What went into the OKR process was often already outdated when we got that far. So the OKRs that came out were too.
>
> We noticed that we were putting energy into a process that wasn't adding value. So we decided to ditch it and focus on context and priorities instead. We make sure everyone knows exactly where we are going and what the current priorities are, and then we let the teams take responsibility for how to get there.[11]

This sounds remarkably aligned with the RPT approach of defining a clear vision and strategy and translating it into priorities and execution.

Ironically, setting performance goals and OKRs can drive pursuits of local maxima and distract us from finding the global maximum. It's time to abandon the approach of using product metrics to set performance goals. It's time for a more radical approach.

MEASUREMENT THE RPT WAY

The RPT approach to measurement is designed as a collaborative approach to help your team to continuously learn and improve your product in an ethical manner. This means aligning the team on what metrics indicate whether your product is creating the change you intended and then managing progress through regular feedback.

OKRs too were intended to create alignment by quantifying the impact the organization strives to create. Most organizations have broad vision statements and haven't yet transitioned to Radical Vision Statements. In the absence of a detailed vision, OKRs offer a detailed narrative of the desired impact, but these come with side effects. To achieve the same alignment without the side effects of goal setting, start by creating a Radical Vision Statement.

The RPT approach to crafting a vision gives teams a clear picture of the world you're collectively bringing about, and the RDCL strategy helps you translate that vision into an actionable plan. You can use the vision and strategy to align the team on the direction and magnitude of the change you want to bring about. By running these cocreation sessions as group exercises, you'll have the team's participation and buy-in on where you're going.

Once you have a clear vision and strategy, you can list the key metrics that would indicate progress—just refrain from setting targets. Periodically you'll need to review whether these metrics continue to be the right ones to measure.

If you're changing from measuring popular metrics to what's right for your organization, you may need to educate your team and investors on how you measure success. It's easy to fall prey to setting your measurement strategy based on how investors or stakeholders might define *traction*. In an organization where *ease of use* was defined as "anything should be one click away," the team had developed a website where any information you needed was one click away on the home page—if you could find it, that is.

When the team built a replacement for this product that organized information well, many elements that used to be on the home page were moved behind a tiered menu. Success for us wasn't about the number of clicks it took users to find what they were looking for but whether people spent less time on the site because they found what they needed very quickly. In making these changes, we needed to communicate a change in how we were measuring success. This alignment is also important because measurement costs time and resources—both to build the ability to capture the data and analyze the data when it becomes available.

Once you have alignment on what to measure, you can begin to share and discuss product metrics. Organizations often use OKRs to assign responsibility for achieving specific metrics and to hold people accountable for outcomes. To achieve accountability without the adverse side effects of a goals-based approach, you can have product teams present product KPIs at regularly scheduled update meetings.

It's important to create a collaborative setting where you celebrate successes and, equally importantly, where teams feel comfortable in openly sharing what could be improved and build on one another's ideas.

Teams have more stats and inside knowledge on their product than higher-level management—if teams feel like they're going to be punished for the metrics they present, managers will get only a selective exposure to favorable metrics or overstated results. Creating a collaborative setting for an open discussion around metrics requires a culture with psychological safety that encourages learning behavior (more on this in the next chapter).

To create such a setting, managers can give teams regular feedback on metrics instead of managing progress by setting goals for what the team should achieve. You'll need to develop a joint understanding of the baseline metrics today and talk about what improvements you want to see, how fast you want to see those improvements, and how that affects priorities. While goal setting and management by objectives are analogous to an end-of-the-year exam, regular feedback cycles throughout the year create opportunities for continuous learning.

Teams that use OKRs spend long hours negotiating these goals. Instead, you can allocate those same hours to regularly scheduled cross-functional discussions where teams present metrics, share their learnings, and get feedback and suggestions from others across the organization. These discussions achieve increased alignment as well as accountability.

Lisa Ordóñez, the lead researcher on "Goals Gone Wild," is now the dean of the Rady School of Management at the University of

California, San Diego. Even with her administrative responsibilities, she has kept up with academic research on goal setting and shared the following with me after reading about the RPT approach to measurement: "My research has revealed the negative impact of goal setting, especially in promoting unethical behavior. One reaction might be to eliminate goals and metrics entirely. However, the Radical Product Thinking approach to measurement allows organizations to align priorities and use metrics in a productive way. It retains the best part of goal setting (directing and aligning actions) without the negative aspects."

Your product is your constantly improving mechanism to bring about the change you envision in the world. Radical Product Thinking helps you deeply connect your execution and measurement to your vision and strategy so you can bring about that constant improvement. In the next chapter, we'll talk about how you can use this new way of thinking to cultivate a culture that facilitates building vision-driven products.

KEY TAKEAWAYS

- In the Radical Product Thinking way, vision and strategy drive hypothesis-driven execution and measurement. Instead of measuring what's popular, measure what's right for your organization.
- This means creating a series of hypotheses and setting up experiments to validate your vision and RDCL strategy.
- RPT is often used together with Lean and Agile methodologies.
- The execution and measurement template includes three elements:
  1. *Key metrics:* These are the key indicators of whether your approach is working.

- Think about what metrics indicate progress toward your vision.
- What metrics will you measure to know if each element of your RDCL strategy is working?

2. *Hypotheses:* Your hypothesis identifies the connection between what you deliver and the metric.
   - You can write a hypothesis using the following Mad Libs statement: If [*experiment*], then [*outcome*], because [*connection*].

3. *Activities to set up the experiment:* In this section of the template you can identify the tasks needed to set up your experiment.
   - If you're using an Agile development process, these activities drive your Agile Sprint.

- Setting goals for product metrics is tempting, but you must resist. The RPT way is a collaborative approach to measure and learn as a team.
- To align your team on metrics and replace goal setting through OKRs, you can take these three practical steps:

1. Align on what you'll measure.
2. Create a safe environment to discuss metrics.
3. Manage progress through regular feedback.

CHAPTER 7

CULTURE
Radical Product Thinking
Your Organization

To build vision-driven products, you need a culture that maximizes intrinsic motivation in employees. In their everyday work, employees repeatedly face the choice of taking shortcuts or putting in more effort; they have to choose between accumulating vision debt and investing in the vision. Motivated employees are more likely to invest in your collective vision.

While the importance of motivated employees is clear, the problem with organizational culture is so pervasive that according to a 2019 Gallup study that surveyed over 12,600 full-time employees, 76 percent of employees reported experiencing burnout on the job at least sometimes, and 28 percent said they felt burned out "very often" or "always" at work.[1]

Until now, organizations have often adopted reactive solutions to culture problems including free snacks, beanbags, meditation classes, and sleep pods. While they may help take the edge off difficult workplaces, with more employees working remotely, these are not universally relevant perks that help with employee well-being or stress reduction. Working remotely accentuates the importance of company culture, and organizations will need a more authentic approach to address cultural issues and keep employees engaged.

Now that you're familiar with the Radical Product Thinking elements of vision, strategy, prioritization, and execution and measurement, you can apply these same ideas to your organizational culture.

In the RPT mindset, you could think of your culture as a product: a mechanism for creating an environment that maximizes intrinsic motivation and helps high-performing teams thrive. Framing culture as a product helps you take a systematic approach to engineer the change you envision.

By now you know the drill! To work on your culture, you need a clear definition of the problem and why the status quo needs to be changed; you need a vision. You can then translate your vision into an actionable plan through a RDCL strategy. Led by this clear vision and strategy for culture change, you'll be able to implement changes and measure progress so you can iterate and make constant improvements.

While this sounds logical, try mentioning culture change in any organization and you'll typically get eye rolls in response. The problem is that culture feels amorphous and is typically defined as the experiences, philosophy, values, beliefs, and customs that hold an organization together. As a result, until now a vision for culture change has been broad and abstract instead of detailed and actionable.

The Radical Product Thinking framework for culture is designed to change this—it helps you structure open and honest discussions with your team to develop a shared understanding of your team culture and develop a clear picture of what needs changing.

As an added benefit, I've found that open discussions using this framework have been a more effective bonding activity for teams than the most memorable off-site I ever attended.

THE RADICAL PRODUCT THINKING FRAMEWORK FOR CULTURE

Articulating your culture starts with the realization that your work culture is the cumulative experience of your workdays and interactions. In the course of your workday, you intuitively engage in work and interactions based on what you find fulfilling versus what floats to the top because it feels urgent. In other words, you experience your workday on two dimensions: how satisfying or depleting it is and whether it feels urgent or not. If you visualize this balance in a two-by-two, as shown in figure 8, the culture you experience is the sum total of how you distribute your mental and emotional bandwidth across four quadrants:

- *Meaningful Work:* This is satisfying work that you do without time pressure. This is where you derive the most enjoyment from your workday.

FIGURE 8: The Radical Product Thinking framework for culture

- *Heroism:* This means doing satisfying work under time pressure. Occasional pressure can add spice to your workday, but too much of it leads to burnout.
- *Organizational Cactus:* This is work that's not fulfilling but comes with some urgency. These are often processes necessary for the organization to function, but too much of these make your workday feel like a walk through a cactus field: painful.
- *Soul-Sucking:* This represents depleting activities that are not urgent—akin to a chronic infection. Examples include managing up or feeling that you were treated unfairly.

A good culture maximizes the time you spend in the Meaningful Work quadrant compared to the other quadrants. This chapter will give you ideas for how you can create an organizational culture that looks like figure 9.

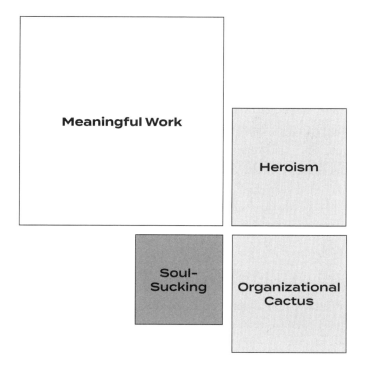

FIGURE 9: A good work culture maximizes the Meaningful Work quadrant and minimizes the others

Meaningful Work

If you spend a lot of your day in the Meaningful Work quadrant, your workplace culture feels meaningful and fulfilling. Maximizing time in this quadrant helps keep employees engaged and able to bring their whole selves to work.

In my culture workshops, I often hear the following examples of what activities make work feel meaningful for individuals:

- Solving a hard problem, feeling like you've achieved something
- Seeing changes or seeing progress
- Working in a team where you feel a strong sense of belonging

Essentially, work that feels like deliberate progress toward your vision of creating a positive change in the world falls in the Meaningful Work quadrant. Activities in the Meaningful Work quadrant are consistent with the three elements of intrinsic motivation described by author Daniel Pink in his bestselling book *Drive: The Surprising Truth about What Motivates Us.*[2] The RPT methodology helps you maximize intrinsic motivation and maps into the elements in *Drive* as shown in table 2.

When you're driven by a clear vision and a comprehensive product strategy that's translated into a clear rationale for prioritization and execution, you'll maximize the time you spend in the Meaningful Work quadrant. On the other hand, without a clear direction, individuals often divert their attention to the next quadrant (Heroism) because it feels urgent and more needed.

Heroism

Work in the Heroism quadrant feels satisfying, but it's under high time pressure. You may have experienced work in this quadrant if you have done any of the following:

TABLE 2. How to use RPT to maximize intrinsic motivation

Drive	Radical Product Thinking
Purpose—the yearning to be part of something larger than ourselves	In contrast to being iteration-led, RPT helps you be purpose-driven and start with a clear vision and strategy to drive your iterations.
Autonomy—the desire to direct our own lives	The RPT rubric for prioritization and decision-making aligns teams on balancing progress toward the vision versus making short-term gains—it's a tool to develop intuition and autonomy. Even when autonomy is not possible, the rubric serves as a communication tool to share your rationale and increase individuals' *perceived* level of autonomy.
Mastery—the urge to make progress on something that matters	The RPT approach of hypothesis-driven execution and measurement helps you monitor progress toward the purpose you defined in your vision and strategy. You use metrics as a learning tool to make continuous improvements.

- Firefighting to fix an urgent customer issue
- Taking on an unmanageable workload because a colleague quit recently and is yet to be replaced
- Pulling a 70-hour workweek coordinating all the activities for your upcoming product launch

Heroism can give an exciting pace to your workday when the time pressure is occasional, but too much time in this quadrant puts you on the fast track to burnout.

Corporate culture frequently incentivizes employees to spend time in this quadrant. At a company where I worked, engineers were praised for spending the night at the customer site fixing issues and rescuing the customer. As a result, engineers learned that to get visibility and advance in their careers, they were better off volunteering for rescue missions instead of dedicating themselves to projects that prevented these issues in the first place.

The demand for heroism in corporate culture can even sound inspirational. In her book, *Uncanny Valley*, Anna Wiener describes the work environment at an analytics startup where the ultimate praise from the CEO was saying an employee was "Down for the Cause or DFTC."[3] Employees earned this praise through extraordinarily long work hours or personal sacrifices. I have heard a similar version at a company where employees proclaimed their loyalty saying, "I bleed [*logo color*]."

The reality is that being down for the cause or bleeding your logo color detracts from the time you'd spend on strategic long-term work. It's also not sustainable. The Gallup study on burnout found that people who report having an unmanageable workload are 2.2 times more likely to report feeling burnout very often or always at work. Similarly, the study found that those who report feeling unreasonable time pressure in their work deadlines are 70 percent more likely to burn out.[4]

To address the Heroism quadrant, we need to ensure that the workload and the time pressure feel sustainable. This may require changing incentives or the reward structure to decrease time in this quadrant.

Organizational Cactus

Organizational Cactus inflicts pain through administrative tasks that don't feel meaningful and don't help you make progress toward the vision, but feel urgent. Examples of Organizational Cactus include the following:

- Filling out long and tedious administrative paperwork for requesting a new laptop
- Requiring approval from many layers of management

- Having to engage in back-channel diplomacy to build consensus across a large group on relatively minor decisions
- Creating reports and dedicating time to metrics that aren't useful indicators of progress

The effect of Organizational Cactus is that your organization feels sluggish. If you can reduce the time spent in this quadrant, you have more bandwidth to spend on meaningful work.

Organizational Cactus can also come in the form of process-heavy workflows in large organizations. These processes can help organizations create consistency in how a task is done so that it can be replicated with precision at scale. For example, in a government organization, having a clear step-by-step process for approving a permit gives applicants predictable and repeatable results at scale. However, the more processes you have that are deeply ingrained, the more "organizational immunity" you have, which creates a strong antibody reaction to any change.

As a result, to embark on culture change when you see a large Organizational Cactus quadrant, you need to get to the root cause of each issue so you can build deep conviction in your team on the core problem (not just the symptom) and plan for how you'll overcome organizational immunity.

For example, in a company where meetings frequently ran long, employees shared their frustration that they spent a lot of time waiting for meetings to start because team members were stuck in other meetings that were overrunning by unpredictable amounts. We could have treated the symptom by getting teams to embrace meeting-management best practices and even enforcing hard cutoff times. However, after observing several meetings, it turned out that the root cause of meeting overruns was the lack of alignment. When individuals started far apart, it was hard for them to come to an agreement on important issues in the span of an hour (or even two hours). The solution we agreed on was to conduct visioning and strategy discussions at an organizational level before introducing best practices for meeting management.

To address Organizational Cactus, create a prioritized list of areas where employees feel like they are spending meaningless effort on administrative tasks, permissions, and reporting. You can then create a plan for reducing the time spent in this quadrant.

Soul-Sucking

The work in the Soul-Sucking quadrant is depleting, but it doesn't feel urgent—it depletes your energy slowly over time. Examples of soul-sucking activity include the following:

- Holding back your thoughts when you disagree for fear of repercussions
- Spending time managing up
- Navigating a toxic and aggressive culture
- Feeling like you're being treated unfairly
- Wondering whether your manager will support you in a wider discussion

Frequently, the root cause of toxic behavior in this quadrant is the emphasis in our culture on rewarding individual productivity more than group productivity. When the group performs well because the collective intelligence of the group is higher and they make better decisions, it's hard to attribute that to specific group members and recognize them for it. It seems easier to recognize individuals for their individual work. But surely if we identify and reward individual productivity and create a group of the top performers, then the group performs well, right?

In a TEDTalk, author and serial entrepreneur Margaret Heffernan refers to a study by William Muir at Purdue University to debunk this myth. In Muir's experiment, he created a flock of superchickens by selecting the most productive *individuals* from each cage to breed the next generation of hens. In a parallel experiment, he created a flock of chickens by breeding *all* the chickens in the best performing cages.

He found that in the group of superchickens, productivity plummeted. Only three rickety-looking superchickens in the cage survived because these hyperaggressive hens had pecked the others to death. On the other hand, in the second group, where all the hens from the best cages were bred, productivity increased over generations, and they were laying 160 percent more eggs. The experiment led to the realization that the most productive hen in each cage achieved productivity by suppressing the other chickens' performance. The bottom line is that to increase performance, you want to avoid superchickens.[5]

An MIT study published in *Science* validated this conclusion in organizational behavior. In a study of 699 volunteers, researchers found that the teams that were better at problem solving and demonstrated a higher "collective intelligence" were ones where members contributed more equally rather than letting one or two people dominate the group.[6] In other words, superchickens lowered the team's collective intelligence score.

Anytime we accommodate and allow for superchicken behavior, we're prioritizing individual performance over group productivity. Any superchicken behavior that's not discouraged is silently condoned. New Zealand's All Blacks rugby team, which has dominated the sport with a 77 percent winning record in test-match rugby, has taken a clear stance that superchickens are not welcome on the team. Their mental skills coach, Gilbert Enoka, explained their "no dickheads" policy in an interview with Adidas' GamePlan A, "Often teams put up with [a big ego] because a player has so much talent. We look for early warning signs and wean the big egos out pretty quickly." Because coaches may not see this behavior in players and it may happen off the field, this no-superchicken policy is often enforced by the players themselves. "In our cornerstone philosophies, the team towers above the individual," Enoka explained. "If you don't put the team first, you'll never make it."[7]

To be clear, this doesn't mean that individual performance isn't important. In fact, some elements in the Soul-Sucking quadrant can result from not holding individuals accountable. In a team where discontent was brewing, a discussion structured around the culture rubric revealed that many of the team members felt that they had to tiptoe around others who weren't pulling their weight. The manager, who had a nonconfrontational style, was avoiding an uncomfortable discussion and wasn't addressing individual performance issues. As a result, those who worked hard and were passionate about the product felt like they were treated unfairly when they had to take on work to make up for those who weren't pulling their weight.

Reducing the size of the Soul-Sucking quadrant comes from finding the right balance between individual and group performance and reducing experiences that gnaw at us by seeming unfair.

HOW TO USE THE CULTURE RUBRIC

Once you begin to see culture as a cumulative set of experiences through your workday, you realize that culture is not just what you intend but how people experience and perceive it. A good culture maximizes the Meaningful Work quadrant and minimizes the time spent in the other three.

This rubric helps you structure a discussion with your team to understand how their time is distributed across the four quadrants. Such a discussion would uncover what makes their work feel meaningful, which activities require too much Heroism from them, which tasks they would characterize as Organizational Cactus, and which interactions feel Soul-Sucking.

A characteristic of high-performing teams is the ability to have these honest and (most likely) uncomfortable discussions so that you're able to align as a team on the problem at hand and come up with solutions. Without such alignment, culture change initiatives and training often feel like additional work without the promise of a clear benefit.

Once you have a clear picture of your culture and what elements of your culture you need to address, you can create an actionable plan by crafting a RDCL strategy. For example, at a company where engineers were experiencing burnout, we used the RDCL strategy to engineer a smaller Heroism quadrant. Here were the elements of our RDCL strategy to tackle the biggest factor that was causing burnout at the time:

- *Real pain point:* With every new product release, our engineers often spent weeks firefighting bugs at the customer site. It was causing people to burn out, and we were going to lose talent if we didn't fix this issue soon.
- *Design:* To solve the above pain point, we realized that we needed to find these bugs before we shipped our hardware and software to the customer site. We began to stage our equipment and test the system by replicating the customer's workflow before shipping the equipment to the site.
- *Capabilities:* We invested in more testing automation so that we could find bugs more efficiently without adding a large head count to our testing team. We also realized that we had to augment our local customer service team's capabilities so that the local team could take on more of the support without requiring engineers to travel to the site.
- *Logistics:* We had to change our incentive structure—engineers often had an incentive to be seen as heroes rescuing customers because it gave them visibility, thus improving their career prospects. We began to offer recognition to teams for launching our product at customer sites without requiring any instances of heroism.

By taking this systematic approach, we reduced the size of our Heroism quadrant and continued to improve other sources of pain in each of the danger quadrants.

It's important to note that culture is not monolithic; instead, people across your organization may be experiencing different amounts of time in each of these quadrants. For example, someone reporting to an insecure micromanager may spend a lot of time in the Soul-Sucking quadrant and experience a very different corporate culture from someone who has a great manager. You could consider anonymous surveys and look at the distribution of responses across departments and managers to gain clues on which leaders may benefit from coaching. Similarly, a view of the response distribution by race, gender, religion, and disability may point to whether a team would benefit from diversity and inclusion efforts.

THE IMPORTANCE OF DIVERSITY AND HOW THE DANGER QUADRANTS AFFECT MINORITIES

Creating a diverse team makes good economic sense. A 2015 McKinsey report on 366 public companies found that those in the top quartile for ethnic and racial diversity in management were 35 percent more likely to deliver above-average financial returns.[8] As a corollary, the dangers of homogeneity in teams is also illustrated by publicly documented product failures. A viral YouTube video illustrates a white person stepping in to help trigger a motion-sensing soap dispenser that didn't recognize the darker palms of a Black person, Google's Photos app was widely criticized for tagging Black people as gorillas. The list of design fails, unfortunately, is long, and so is the list of companies where people of color are vastly underrepresented.

To create products that work for our diverse society, not only do we need diversity on our teams, but we also need to engineer a culture where people of any color, gender, and ethnicity can do their best work together. The tech industry has often focused on the pipeline problem and hiring for diversity. But once we look at the four quadrants of culture, it becomes clear that addressing the lack of diversity in hiring is necessary but not enough.

People of color often experience more events of unfairness that increase the time they spend in the Soul-Sucking quadrant. A 2017 Pew Research Center survey found that roughly 62 percent of Black STEM (science, technology, engineering, and math) workers say they have experienced racial or ethnic discrimination at work, from earning less than a coworker who performed the same job to experiencing repeated small slights at work. That compares with 44 percent of Asians, 42 percent of Hispanics, and 13 percent of whites in STEM jobs.[9] Data confirms the unfairness in the pay gap—for example, in 2018, among full-time workers, Black women earned 61.9 cents for every dollar that white men earned.[10]

People of color often have to counter a common bias in the STEM field that they are less competent. According to a Pew Research Center report, "Among STEM employees, 45 percent of blacks say they have had this experience because of their race or ethnicity, compared with smaller shares of Hispanics (23 percent), Asians (20 percent), and whites (3 percent)."[11] As a result, Black people may feel compelled to work harder to overcome such stereotypes and are likely to spend more time in the Heroism quadrant where everything feels high stakes and they're constantly judged.

Similarly, these biases may mean that they're given less responsibility and their talents aren't fully utilized. As a result, they may be spending less time in the Meaningful Work quadrant. They may be taking on more of the administrative tasks or grunt work that their colleagues may not have to take on, thus adding to their activities in the Organizational Cactus quadrant.

The end effect is that minorities often experience a culture that looks like figure 10.

If you're talking about these quadrants at work, you'll need to be aware that minorities are feeling a bigger effect from the danger quadrants than other employees. But these are hard conversations to have in the workplace. A great reference on how to have these conversations is Mary-Frances Winters's *Inclusive Conversations: Fostering Equity, Empathy, and Belonging across Differences.*

Having these conversations is an important start, but if those discussions are not followed by actions, your team will find these discussions inauthentic and hollow. You'll need to have regular check-ins as you take action and evolve your culture through iterations.

To deliver on Khan Academy's vision of creating a world-class education for anyone, anywhere, May-Li Khoe, former vice president

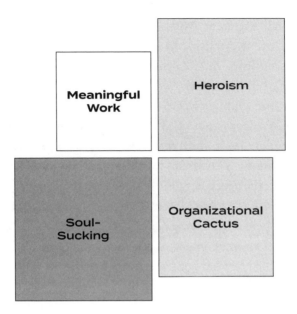

FIGURE 10: The culture minorities often experience

of design, recognized that it was important for her team to be as diverse as the website's users. Khoe designed a weekly survey that's reminiscent of the four quadrants to measure whether her diverse team had the environment where they could do their best work together. She shared with me her survey that had just five statements:

- I feel valued on this team.
- I have the opportunity to learn and grow on this team.
- I have the support I need to be successful on this team.
- I worked sustainably last week.
- I'm proud of the work I'm doing.

Her actions consistently demonstrated that the weekly survey had real ramifications. For example, if people were working unsustainably, she'd use the data in cross-functional meetings to advocate for adjusting project plans so heroism didn't become a regular way of working.

Khoe also worked to avoid unfair practices such as pay gaps on her team. Women and minorities often have less perceived (or real) leverage in negotiations and may not negotiate their starting pay. Khoe's offer letters were based on paying people market rates, and she set expectations with candidates that the offer was deliberately designed to be nonnegotiable to avoid a pay gap. Because of this system, in some instances, people from traditionally underpaid groups were offered salaries substantially above their expectations. This is one example of a strategy to reduce the size of the Soul-Sucking quadrant.

THE IMPORTANCE OF PSYCHOLOGICAL SAFETY

Talking openly about Meaningful Work, Heroism, Organizational Cactus, and Soul-Sucking activities is easier in an environment that allows for such open and honest dialogue. Indeed, such an environment will make it much easier to use the RPT approach in a team. For example, when crafting a vision and strategy you need diverse opinions to challenge and refine ideas. You're also more likely to communicate your decision-making rationale and use metrics as a learning tool when it's easy to have direct and collaborative discussions.

One of the most memorable group collaborations I've experienced was when I was working with Geordie Kaytes and Nidhi Aggarwal to create the Radical Product Thinking framework. We had a deep mutual respect for the unique perspectives we brought, and this meant we could be ourselves. Any of us could share a half-baked idea—in fact, it often formed the kernel that the others built on. For example, I process information verbally, and thinking out loud helps me refine my ideas. This meant that in our meetings I felt free to share a perspective and correct myself, or even withdraw the idea, as I explained it in more detail. Our whiteboard sessions felt like a mind meld—you couldn't tell who came up with which idea. We were displaying learning behavior as a team.

The sense of confidence that the team will not penalize or think less of someone for making a mistake or asking for help, information, or feedback is what Amy Edmondson, Harvard Business School professor, termed *psychological safety* in her research in 1999.[12] In a study of medical teams performing a complex cardiac procedure using new technology, she found that in the teams with the best outcomes, all members involved in the procedure (regardless of their seniority or stature) felt free to say something if they thought something was going wrong or if they had an idea that would solve a problem.[13]

As a result, teams with psychological safety also innovated better. For example, one nurse spontaneously came up with an idea to solve a problem by using a long-forgotten clamp called the "iron intern," and it became part of the team's regular process. Other teams without psychological safety didn't innovate new processes even when a team member noticed opportunities for improvement.

Psychological safety gave team members the confidence to take interpersonal risks, leading to learning behavior, which in turn led to better performance.

But although it's clear that psychological safety is important for teams, it's not as common as it should be. I think back to my days at Avid and remember an example that shows how the management team consciously created psychological safety in the team.

Just a few months into my new job at Avid, I was in a monthly strategy meeting with the chief executives, including Mike Rockwell, who was the CTO at the time and now leads the augmented and virtual reality effort at Apple. I described a customer's feature request that Rockwell thought we already had. I remember debating this with him to explain why that was not the case and outline the engineering effort that was needed. Not only did Rockwell encourage the debate, but he concluded that I was right.

What was unusual about this interaction was that I was barely six months into the job, and while I had technical chops, I wasn't a software engineer—yet I could have a technical debate with the CTO and be heard. That was psychological safety.

Psychological safety starts with reducing the socio-emotional risk of admitting mistakes. As humans, we go to great lengths to save face and avoid admitting to a mistake. Rockwell could have easily avoided saying that I was right, but by saying so deliberately, he made it acceptable for other leaders in that meeting to be fallible.

He also encouraged a direct debate—I didn't have to tiptoe around the issue and worry about contradicting him. As a result, we could discuss the details quickly and make a decision. What he modeled was the culture of caring personally and therefore challenging directly, something author Kim Scott calls "radical candor."[14]

Radical candor, however, was possible only because I didn't face the risk that this was a rare interaction with Rockwell. If this had been the only time we were going to interact, I may have felt the need to be more guarded and not risk being perceived as a "know-it-all." At Avid, the executives had an open-door policy that felt genuine. Our broadcast group usually had lunch together in the cafeteria and occasionally Rockwell joined us too. Accessibility laid the foundation for radical candor and psychological safety.

The management team at Avid created psychological safety by reinforcing it regularly in interactions. The result is that 15 years later I still recall the joy of working together as we were building our broadcast business.

The Radical Product Thinking approach to culture gives you a systematic approach to engineer the environment your team needs to solve hard problems and build successful products: one that maximizes intrinsic motivation and minimizes anything that detracts from it. The RPT rubric for culture gives you a framework for having conversations so you can articulate the culture your team experiences and create an actionable plan (a strategy) for what needs changing. If we want our successful products to create a better world for all, then in addition to having a clear vision, strategy, and execution, we must create a workplace that works for everyone in our organization.

KEY TAKEAWAYS

- In the Radical Product Thinking way, culture can be your product: your mechanism for creating an environment that maximizes intrinsic motivation and minimizes anything that detracts from it.
- You can think of your culture as the cumulative set of your experiences during your workday.
- The RPT rubric for culture helps you see your workday along two dimensions: whether work is satisfying or depleting and whether it's urgent or not. The rubric reveals the following four quadrants:
  1. *Meaningful Work:* Satisfying but not urgent work that makes you feel like you're making progress toward a larger purpose
  2. *Heroism:* Satisfying work that's urgent and adds spice to your workday but can lead to burnout
  3. *Organizational Cactus:* Tasks that are depleting but urgent; some amount is necessary in any organization, but too much is painful
  4. *Soul-Sucking:* Depleting and not urgent work that slowly sucks energy out of you
- This framework helps you develop a clear vision for your culture: making the Meaningful Work quadrant larger and the danger quadrants smaller.
- Understanding the activities in each quadrant is key to crafting a RDCL strategy to address the root cause behind the time spent in each of the danger quadrants.
- To create diversity on a team, you need to acknowledge that people of color are most likely experiencing a culture where the danger quadrants are larger than the Meaningful Work quadrant.

- A good organizational culture has psychological safety, which can be deliberately created by modeling the following:
  - *Fallibility:* Making it okay to be wrong and to learn from mistakes
  - *Direct communication:* Caring personally and therefore challenging directly
  - *Accessibility:* Increasing the frequency of interactions so that it's easier to take interpersonal risks

PART III

MAKING OUR WORLD A LITTLE MORE LIKE THE ONE WE WANT TO LIVE IN

CHAPTER 8

DIGITAL POLLUTION

The Collateral Damage
to Society

I teration-led products find local maxima by optimizing financial metrics, but in the process, they often have unintended consequences on society. The iteration-led approach is so common that we have learned to accept a dichotomy: you can be successful, or you can make the world a better place.

We see mounting evidence of a generation of disillusioned employees in the technology industry coming to terms with this dichotomy. Employees at Google and Amazon have staged walkouts to protest how their employers' products and practices are failing society.[1] *Uncanny Valley*, the memoir of a young professional trying to find meaningful work in the tech industry, became a *New York Times* bestseller. Websites like Tech for Good offer tech employees sparse hope that they can still find work that doesn't spark an overwhelming desire to wash one's conscience afterward.[2]

These examples reflect the growing dissatisfaction of the cohort that entered the tech industry inspired by the vision that technology and innovation were going to change the world. For a while, the sheer volume of products and startups launched made the change seem like progress. But recent studies show that technology hasn't always made the world better.[3]

Here's a personal example of what sounded like a promising innovation. When my son was seven, he came home from school excited about a game, Prodigy, that he had played at school. His math teacher had introduced it to the advanced math students in his class as a way to keep them engaged. It was popular among his friends too, and he was begging me to play it. It turned out that my daughter, who was 10 at the time and also an advanced math student, had also been introduced to Prodigy. She, however, didn't share her brother's enthusiasm for the product.

As I watched the gameplay in Prodigy, it was soon apparent why—the game lets you pick your character (reminiscent of Pokémon) and attack your opponent by answering math questions correctly. The gameplay seemed to be clearly targeted at boys. Studies have shown that the motivation behind playing video games differs by gender: while boys frequently want to compete (duels, matches) and use guns and explosives in the game, most girls' primary motivations are completion (collectibles, completion of all missions) and immersing themselves in other worlds.[4] This difference was playing out in how my kids perceived the game—even Prodigy's marketing video in 2017 showed boys pumping fists while girls were rarely featured in the video, and in the rare seconds that they were, they didn't show the same level of enthusiasm.[5]

Curious to see if my kids thought it was designed with a particular gender in mind, I asked them. "Definitely boys," my son replied. My daughter added with biting sarcasm, "But don't worry, the next version will be for girls and it'll have Disney princesses that invite you to tea if you get the answer right." My 7- and 10-year-olds could see through the gender targeting in the product.

As if to confirm their views on gender stereotypes, a 2018 video on Prodigy's website designed to sell parents on the benefits of membership shows a young boy explaining why he loves learning math on

Prodigy and that he can do all multiplication and division problems easily. "What is 9x9? It's 81. Easy!" he exclaims. This is followed by an enthusiastic little girl's recommendation: "I also love being a member. You could get these new hairstyles, new clothes, those hats, those shoes." She says nothing about learning or math.[6]

A product could target all children equally, without gender stereotypes. Khan Academy purposefully took this approach. Its former vice president of design, May-Li Khoe, explained in our conversation:

> Khan Academy's mission is to provide a free, world-class education for anyone, anywhere. That meant to me that we were working to create a more equitable world. I wanted that lens of equity to permeate all of our work, from hiring to illustration. This required additional effort.
>
> It meant I was spending time ensuring design decisions were made to support that vision, including hiring and mentoring team members to do this. It meant my team and I put work into codifying values and designing processes to entrench the ethos of equity into all of our work, such as establishing photography usage guidelines to combat stereotypes. Often this effort isn't reflected in typical financial metrics, but we knew it affected our brand and potentially any student and teacher who sees our work.

Khan Academy's visual direction is designed to be gender-neutral. Even the names used in word problems were diverse, thanks to the efforts of Khan Academy's content team. While these inclusion efforts may not have *provably* affected financial metrics, they certainly made a positive difference to my daughter.

In pursuit of financial metrics, Prodigy was finding a local maximum—it was effective at teaching boys math (at least my son and his friends). But the byproduct of its approach was propagating gender inequality in the classroom. By leaving out the girls in the classroom, it was missing out on the global maximum. Khan Academy was taking a vision-driven approach to find the global maximum.

In building our products, we're constantly making choices to either find the global maximum or settle for local maxima. While online education was one example, our products touch most aspects of people's lives including how we stay connected with friends, whom we choose to date,[7] whether we get access to credit,[8] whether we see a job ad,[9] whether we get called for a job interview,[10] and even how we may be judged by a court of law.[11] In each of these cases, our products produce benefits for some while creating collateral damage.

We know how fossil fuels and other byproducts of the industrial age have affected people's health and contributed to the climate crisis. In the digital era, a new kind of pollution, fueled by carefree growth in the tech industry, is having an unintended yet profound impact on society. This emerging trend of inflicting collateral damage through our products is what I call *digital pollution*. But as with any new form of pollution, recognizing it takes time. To build our businesses and develop our products more responsibly, we must be able to recognize and understand the effects of digital pollution, which can be broadly categorized into five categories.

FUELING INEQUALITY

Fueling inequality is a common form of pollution as innate biases permeate into the product, mirroring and amplifying stereotypes in society. Prodigy is an example of digital pollution that exacerbates gender inequality in STEM education.

Increasing inequality is a growing threat to society as artificial intelligence (AI) becomes more pervasive in products. Timnit Gebru, renowned researcher in ethical AI, was ousted from Google in 2020 after writing a paper that pinpointed flaws in the company's language models that underpin its search engine. The system uses large amounts of text from online sources including Wikipedia entries, online books, and articles that often include biased and hateful language. Her research pointed out that a system trained to normalize such language would perpetuate its use.[12]

Gebru was arguing for more thoughtful training models for AI and the need for a more vision-driven approach to AI to prevent this form of pollution.

In addition to fueling inequality through biases in products, business practices can also increase inequality. The digital economy has increased wealth inequality to levels not seen since the Great Depression.[13] For decades, through deunionization and outsourcing, the risk of economic downturns has been shifted from companies to workers. The pendulum has swung from lifetime employment with well-funded pension plans to the gig economy where workers typically don't have health insurance. Companies hire workers as and when they are needed—any risk with an economic downturn or a decrease in demand is borne by the workers.[14]

Economists who believed that the weakening of labor laws would spur growth in the tech sector and, in turn, lead to better pay for workers are realizing that this may no longer be true.[15] According to researchers, employment has fallen in every industry that used technology to increase productivity.[16] Essentially, automation is pushing workers to lower-paying jobs in the economy.

In the same timeframe, share buybacks have reached record levels, predominantly benefiting shareholders and executives.[17] Increasing inequality makes people more disillusioned with majority rule.[18] Products that increase inequality are contributing to digital pollution by creating an increasingly divisive society that destabilizes society.[19]

HIJACKING ATTENTION

In his essay in 1997, theoretical physicist Michael Goldhaber popularized the term *attention economy*, where every company, influencer, and entity vies for the one finite resource: your attention.[20] Each email, alert, or notification does its part in trying to hijack your attention for just an instant, keeping you in a constant state of alert, afraid of missing out. Repeated attention hijacking has two detrimental effects.

First, to maintain this hyperalert state, the human body releases the stress hormones adrenaline and cortisol—several studies have illustrated the correlation between increased smartphone use and higher stress levels.[21] While these mechanisms help us cope with stress in the short term, high levels of these stress hormones circulating in the body over the long term have a detrimental effect on health and mental well-being. Research shows that these high levels have an inflammatory effect on brain cells and are linked to depression.[22]

Second, the repeated dispersion of our attention reduces our ability to interpret and analyze the deeper meaning of information. Studies show that heavy users of the internet use shallow processing—scanning information to get a breadth of information but at a superficial level.[23] If we're not able to get to the deeper meaning of things, it's easy to latch onto sound bites but harder to process nuance.

Society thrives on nuance. But increasingly nuance, like attention, is scarce. To understand why society needs nuance, consider the example of South Africa's transition from apartheid to democracy in the early '90s. There were extremist factions: some white supremacist leaders incited followers to take up arms to protect their privilege and property, while some Black leaders wanted payback for the atrocities of apartheid. This could have been the beginning of a descent into violence, but Nelson Mandela and F. W. de Klerk inspired the country with a shared vision. They initiated a Truth and Reconciliation Commission to acknowledge the atrocities and to begin to make amends. Their nuanced but inspiring message resonated with the population, and South Africa made a peaceful transition to democracy.

In contrast, President George W. Bush famously said, "I don't do nuance," when making the case for going to war in Iraq after 9/11. Instead the argument was a set of frequently repeated sound bites that Saddam Hussein was dangerous and was acquiring nuclear weapons.

For society to function, people need the mental bandwidth and attention to be able to absorb nuance and not just sound bites. Products designed to hijack users' attention create digital pollution by eroding our ability to absorb information.

CREATING IDEOLOGICAL POLARIZATION

Rising inequality and attention dispersion create a fertile ground for ideological polarization. While there are several underlying reasons for political polarization, including the rise of partisan cable news, changing political party composition, and racial divisions, digital products also contribute to the polarization effect.

With attention being a scarce resource, a frequently used technique to increase user engagement is to make users crave validation in the form of "follows," "likes," and "faves." Studies show that this desire for validation leads people to post increasingly polarizing content and to express moral outrage.[24]

Algorithms too are increasingly contributing to polarization. YouTube, for example, introduced an algorithm in 2012 to recommend and autoplay videos that has worked exceedingly well and accounts for 70 percent of time spent by users on the site.[25]

In the process, however, YouTube has fueled conspiracy theories and radicalization online.[26] Each subsequent recommendation by the platform pushes you toward a more extreme view—for example, if you start looking at videos about nutrition, after a few videos you end with recommendations on extreme dieting videos. This is now termed the *rabbit-hole effect*.[27]

Ex-employee Guillaume Chaslot, who worked on this algorithm, explains this effect of radicalization in a blog post. The algorithm creates a vicious cycle. For example, some people may click on a flat-earth video out of curiosity, but because the video was engaging, it gets recommended millions of times and gets millions of views. As it gets more views, more people watch it, and some believe that it must be true if it has gotten so many views and distrust mainstream media that doesn't share this "important" information with them. As a result, they spend more time on YouTube and watch more conspiracy theory videos.

In effect, the smart AI algorithm increases engagement on its platform by discrediting other media. When other media channels are discredited, engagement with YouTube increases.[28]

Chaslot found this same recurring theme of "the media is lying" when analyzing YouTube recommendations. In the 2016 elections, YouTube was four times more likely to recommend the candidate who was most aggressively critical of the media. Similarly, the three most recommended candidates in the French election of 2017 were the ones who were most critical of the media.[29]

Products that increase ideological polarization create digital pollution by increasing divisions and amplifying distrust in society.

ERODING PRIVACY

As the cost of data storage has decreased exponentially over the years and the value of personal data has become evident from company valuations, it's tempting to amass user data when building products. When there's doubt about whether a specific type of user data is necessary, it feels smarter to err on the side of collecting this data. It might pay off later. For example, a big reason WhatsApp was so valuable to Facebook was that the firm stored data on who called whom and when, data on offline relationships that Facebook wasn't privy to through its platform.[30]

Personal data helps us build better products and can help us learn more about our users and customize our offering for them. But personal data can also be used to influence individuals' decisions, manipulate their behavior, and affect their reputation.

Most of us who build products are also consumers who are asked to make the all-too-frequent trade-off of using a free product in exchange for our personal data. Giving up personal data has become normalized to the point that we often justify giving away our data saying, "I have nothing to hide." It's natural to bring this consumer mindset into building products and err on the side of collecting data.

This approach, however, creates collateral damage to society. Perhaps your personal data doesn't matter. But what if authorities can thwart change by using personal data on human rights activists or journalists to intimidate or discredit them? Erosion of privacy erodes democracy.

Privacy cannot be for the few—it's not possible to protect the personal data of just a few individuals whose data can be used against them. Privacy is either for everyone or for no one. The few whose data really matters cannot be the only ones who advocate for privacy.

Society is worse off if we don't value privacy enough to make it standard to protect everyone's personal data.

When we think about it this way, privacy is not just a right; it's also a responsibility. We need a vision-driven approach to collecting and storing data to avoid digital pollution in the form of erosion of privacy.

ERODING THE INFORMATION ECOSYSTEM

The early days of the internet in the 1990s and early 2000s offered promise and hope for democratizing knowledge across the globe—anyone looking for information could have it at one's fingertips. But in recent decades, as social media and platforms have transformed how we share and distribute information, we're seeing how truth itself can be disrupted through disinformation.

During a cab ride recently, the conversation with my driver, Vincent, turned to politics. He shared the news that he had read about various politicians, but each time he added a disclaimer: "This is what I read, but who knows if it's true." His most sobering comment spoke to the erosion of our information ecosystem and the alarming spread of disinformation: "Years ago, I would open a newspaper and feel like I got the facts. Today, I have access to all the information I want, but I just don't know what is real."

Some of the most prominent, widely used products in the digital era have eroded our access to knowledge and facts. For example, we instinctively Google the answer to any question that might come up in a conversation. But while Google offers a powerful search tool so information is at your fingertips, its business model essentially allows the highest spender to decide the "truth." Approximately 95 percent of web traffic from a search result goes to the listings on the first page, and few people scroll past the first page of search results. This means if you can spend enough on search engine optimization (SEO) and search result placement, you can generate content that's perceived as the truth by the vast majority of people searching for that topic.[31]

Curating truth has been possible since ancient history. For example, Roman emperors commissioned mythology to be written about their divine origins to justify their birthright to rule. But creating truth required resources; the bar today is much lower.

In pointing out these issues I'm not making the Luddite argument that we were better off before the digital age. But technology and the ubiquity of information isn't a panacea either—the spread of information too requires a vision-driven approach for the world we want to bring about. Products that contribute to eroding the information ecosystem create the paradox that with the abundance of information, gaining knowledge actually becomes harder.

The combined effects of these forms of digital pollution are starting to become evident. With the rising inequality, polarization, attention hijacking, and erosion of privacy and the information ecosystem, manipulating populations en masse becomes easier.

In 2014 Facebook demonstrated through an experiment on over one million users that it was able to make individuals feel positive or negative emotions by curating the content in their newsfeeds.[32] The power of using Facebook for manipulation was known at least as early as 2010 but more fully entered public awareness after the Cambridge Analytica scandal erupted in 2018, illustrating the platform's power in swaying elections.[33]

Together, these forms of pollution fray the fabric of a stable, democratic society. Most of us joined the workforce believing that our innovations could change the world for the better. Given our positive intent, it's especially difficult to reckon with the toll our companies have taken on society.

But we must remember that we had to recognize and label environmental pollution before companies began to consider their impact on the environment and address it. Similarly, only when we recognize digital pollution can we take responsibility for the products we build.

Accepting that our products might be causing digital pollution is often difficult because the underlying product decisions are not deliberately malicious. So how do we create digital pollution when we don't intentionally choose to?

When we're iteration-led, we pursue local maxima by optimizing for only a few chess pieces. We miss out on the best move across the chess board, the global maximum, that accounts for user and societal well-being. In an iteration-led approach we test features in the market to see what customers respond to, and we iterate. But to assess what customers like, we look at financial metrics, typically revenues or time spent on-site. As a result, an iteration-led approach often optimizes for financial metrics without consideration for user or societal well-being.

The iteration-led approach to maximize profitability is often accompanied with the mindset that everything is ripe for disruption: "Disrupt or be disrupted!" But disrupting and "screwing up the status quo"[34] without a clear purpose has often created collateral damage in society.

One example of disruption leading to a worse outcome for society is the long-term assault on the business model of news and journalism in the United States. A study of polarization in nine member countries of the Organization for Economic Co-operation and Development over the past four decades found that the United States experienced the largest increase in polarization over this period. One of the major reasons was the creation of cable news, where the ad-based revenue model requires striving for high viewer ratings and has led to more polarizing content.[35] In fact, the study noted that in countries where political polarization decreased in the same timeframe, public broadcasting received more public funding than it did in the United States. The disruption of the media and broadcast industry illustrates that not all that *can* be disrupted for the sake of profits *should* be.

In building our products while pursuing profits, we can no longer ignore how we impact society. This is not to diminish the importance of pursuing profits. Figure 11 illustrates the intersection between profits and purpose. Companies that optimize for profits without a clear purpose create digital pollution. In contrast, organizations with a clear purpose that disregard profits are operating as charities. Charities

FIGURE 11: The intersection of profitability and purpose

are important but can't carry the entire burden of creating a better world—the business world touches billions more lives than charities. For sustainable growth, society needs more businesses to pursue profits while being vision-driven.

The COVID-19 pandemic has highlighted what's broken in our society. Iteration alone isn't going to fix it—the future demands a vision-driven approach for every product. For example, in the United States the healthcare system is designed on the model that it offers excellent care to those who can afford it. Even before the pandemic, this model was a strain for Americans. As many as 25 percent of Americans were delaying medical care for serious illnesses because of the rising costs[36]—the life expectancy of the wealthiest Americans now exceeds that of the poorest by 10–15 years.[37]

This current business model behind healthcare also leads to a widening economic inequality. Over 137 million Americans reported financial hardship owing to medical bills, and for years, medical debt has been the primary reason for personal bankruptcies.[38] Children in these families have fewer opportunities for education than those raised in families who aren't burdened by medical debt. The unintended consequence of the current healthcare system is that it's perpetuating wealth inequality in the United States. Having read this chapter, you now have a label for this: digital pollution.

Today's healthcare system results from the ideology that a privatized system that relies on free markets will be efficient and good for society—it wasn't driven by a clear vision for healthcare and the end state it creates for society. As a result, the current healthcare system has fallen victim to being iteration-led, and many companies involved have found local maxima by optimizing for profits in the short term. A vision-driven approach to healthcare could, for example, start with an inclusive vision of health as a human right. The "product" of the healthcare system would then need to be designed systematically to bring about that vision.

The 2020s have ushered in a new era that will require us to build products differently. Radical Product Thinking is a new mindset for this era so we can systematically build vision-driven products while creating the change we want to see in the world.

KEY TAKEAWAYS

- Digital pollution is the collateral damage to society from unregulated tech growth, just as environmental pollution is the damage from unregulated industrial growth.
- We may be tempted to think that just a few tech giants create digital pollution. In reality, unintended consequences and digital pollution are pervasive.
- Digital pollution frays the fabric of society in five major ways:
  o Fueling inequality
  o Hijacking attention
  o Creating ideological polarization

- o Eroding privacy
- o Eroding the information ecosystem
- The responsibility of societal well-being cannot fall to charities alone—businesses affect many millions more people.
- You can build vision-driven products that avoid digital pollution—anything can be your product if it is your mechanism to create change.

CHAPTER 9

ETHICS

The Hippocratic
Oath of Product

During the summer of 2017, my family and I were on a road trip through Portugal and we came across a small town, Batalha, where a major attraction was a beautiful Dominican monastery, Mosteiro da Batalha, built in the early 1400s.

One room in particular was an architectural marvel: it had a star-vaulted ceiling spanning 19 square meters with no central support! Architect David Huguet had designed a feature that had never been done before, and the work was so risky that only condemned prisoners were used to build this ceiling. When the vaulted ceiling was finally built after two failed attempts, Huguet had to sleep under it for two nights to prove that it was safe. He had to take responsibility for what he built by risking his life because everyone knew what he was attempting to build was dangerous.

The consequences of building products in tech weren't obvious until now, and as a result, we've often had a callous approach to it, made famous by Facebook's early motto: "Move fast and break things."

Facebook was built on existing, nonrevolutionary technology. It wasn't the underlying technology that was dangerous but the scale of influence it developed that gave it the power to change democracies. Newer platforms are growing their scale of influence even faster than Facebook did.

It took Facebook two years to hit the 50 million user mark. Instagram, which arrived later, reached the same milestone in 19 months by 2016. In comparison, TikTok (founded in 2016) grew to 500 million users in two years. Technologies in the last 50 years touch more lives and faster than they did in the previous 50 years.[1] Figures 12a and 12b show a comparison of technological adoption over the 50 years from 1919 to 1969 and from 1969 to 2019, respectively. The increasing rate of technological adoption fuels an increasing pace at which entities are able to build a scale of influence.

Until the late 19th century, most businesses operated out of a single office or factory in one geographical location. They had limited

Technology adoption in US households, 1919 to 1969

Technology adoption rates, measured as the percentage of households in the United States using a particular technology.

Source: Comin and Hobijn (2004) and others

OurWorldInData.org/technology-adoption/ • CC BY

Note: See the sources tab for definitions of household adoption, or adoption rates, by technology type.

FIGURE 12a: Pace of technology adoption in the 50 years from 1919 to 1969

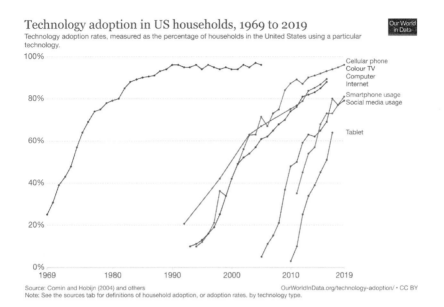

Technology adoption in US households, 1969 to 2019
Technology adoption rates, measured as the percentage of households in the United States using a particular technology.

FIGURE 12b: Pace of technology adoption in the 50 years from 1969 to 2019

influence. Today, companies reach millions of people faster than they ever could before.

We are operating in a world where the technologies and products we create could rapidly affect millions of people in increasingly sophisticated ways. Unlike Huguet's star-vaulted ceiling, we haven't fully understood the consequences of the products we've built, and as a result, we haven't expected the architects to take responsibility for what they built. We're only just beginning to see that without a systematic approach to creating change, we are increasingly changing the world in ways that we didn't intend.

When you innovate, you work to identify a problem and you engineer your product to solve it. A medical doctor does something similar: diagnose the root cause of the patient's condition and treat it. But imagine your doctor says, "I see that you're sick, so I'm going to prescribe this medicine. It may have terrible side effects for you, but that's not my responsibility." Most likely you'd find this attitude appalling. A doctor who can't take responsibility for your well-being has no business treating you.

While this philosophy now seems obvious, it wasn't always so. The Hippocratic oath first appeared around 400 BC, but it wasn't incorporated into medicine until the 1700s. It took time to understand the ethical questions around medicine, the existence of side effects, and the unintended consequences of any treatment.

In building products, we need a Hippocratic oath as much as doctors do. As a society, we're beginning to realize that as with a doctor's work, ethics questions continuously permeate even simple decisions. Ethics questions in the past would bubble up in social consciousness when new technologies were being introduced that could visibly affect humanity—for example, weapons technology or designer babies. Now we're seeing ethics questions permeate our business models and feature decisions even when the underlying technology doesn't seem revolutionary.

Let's take the example of OkCupid, a dating site that has been largely free of controversy. But even OkCupid has found that Black women get disproportionly fewer messages.[2] Most dating sites use collaborative filtering to recommend profiles you're likely to like (similar to how Netflix recommends movies). It turns out that this approach reinforces the biases in our society. When many users don't seem interested in certain profiles, the algorithm stops recommending those profiles to anyone. The choices we make to maximize our product usage and achieve business goals can often trade off a customer's well-being even before we realize it.

Though these trade-offs permeate our businesses, we measure the success of our products by popular financial metrics including revenue and the lifetime value of a customer. The result is that prioritizing profitability over user well-being, and accepting this collateral damage to society, is the norm.

This norm of prioritizing profitability over digital pollution is analogous to littering. Researchers have found that in a littered parking lot, you're more likely to litter too—after all, everyone else is doing it.

A conversation I had with an entrepreneur working on generating a digital replica of a person illustrates this analogy of littering. He was building his product using AI to scan your online existence and create an avatar that one could interact with that would look and sound like you. He was proud to share that this would allow one to also recreate someone who had passed away. When I asked him if he was concerned about the ethics of what he was creating, his answer, unfortunately, was one that I've heard often: "If I don't build it, someone else will."

I've also heard a similar version of this admission of littering positioned as heroism: "At least by building it, we can control it and do the right thing with it. We can be the good guys." Even as WhatsApp founder Jan Koum projected the image of being a champion of privacy, WhatsApp was recording vast amounts of metadata, including whom a user talked to and when.[3] Such metadata has enormous value. For example, even if the content of a conversation is encrypted, metadata revealing that a whistleblower under investigation called a journalist's phone number can be compromising. The founders deluded themselves into thinking that they would collect metadata and yet be able to protect it.[4] They thought of themselves as the good guys even as they sold the company to Facebook.

Often leaders justify not taking responsibility by deflecting it to the users: "Whether I build it or someone else does, the technology is going to exist anyway. So it's the user's responsibility to use it properly." Amazon had pitched Rekognition, its facial recognition platform, to US Immigration and Customs Enforcement (ICE) and put a one-year moratorium on police use of Rekognition only after the Black Lives Matter protests following George Floyd's death. In an interview with the BBC in 2019, Amazon's CTO, Werner Vogels, didn't feel that it was Amazon's responsibility to make sure Rekognition is used accurately or ethically. "This technology is being used for good in many places. It's in society's direction to actually decide which technology is applicable under which conditions," he said.[5]

Some companies take an even more aggressive stance in placing responsibility on the users. Drug company Purdue Pharma, owned by the Sackler family, released OxyContin in 1996. By 2015 their fami-ly's net worth was estimated at $13 billion. To aggressively promote the drug and increase prescription sales, company representatives told doctors that "trustworthy" patients would not get addicted to opioids. To promote prescriptions of higher doses, they created literature about "pseudoaddiction," claiming that if users seem to be getting addicted, it's because they were not getting enough pain relief and needed higher dosages. This claim of pseudoaddiction was not founded in science.

When it became clear in the early 2000s that the opioids were addictive, Purdue Pharma's president at the time, Richard Sackler, advised sales reps to push blame onto people who had become addicted. According to Massachusetts court filings, Sackler wrote in an email in 2001, "We have to hammer on the abusers in every way possible. They are the culprits and the problem. They are reckless criminals."[6] In Purdue's case, blaming users was their dubious justification for littering the market with opioids.

The examples above illustrate that the mindset of "If I don't do it, someone else will" maximizes individual gains at the expense of our well-being as a society. And in the process, it destabilizes society by increasing inequality, polarization, and misinformation—in the long run it creates a suboptimal outcome for all.

PRISONER'S DILEMMA

I've come to realize that the decisions around maximizing individual gains or pursuing collective gains when we build products and scale companies are reminiscent of game theory, specifically, Prisoner's Dilemma, illustrated in figure 13.

Prisoner's Dilemma is a model that's commonly used in eco-nomics and business strategy and demonstrates the incentives and outcomes when we choose between self-interest and mutual benefit. Imagine two criminals who have committed a robbery together but have been arrested on lesser charges and are being held in separate rooms. If they both collaborate and stay silent (the CC quadrant),

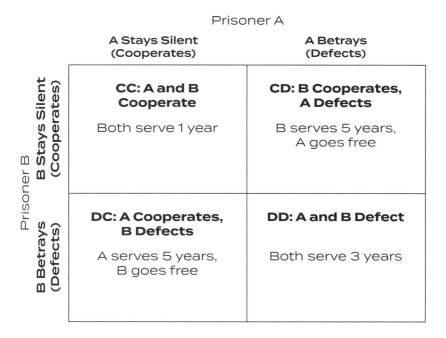

FIGURE 13: Prisoner's Dilemma payoff matrix

each gets a prison sentence of one year on the lesser charge. But each has a strong incentive to defect—each prisoner is told that if he pleads guilty and testifies against the other, he gets immunity while the other receives a harsher five-year sentence. If both end up defecting (DD quadrant), neither gets immunity and each gets a longer sentence of three years. To maximize collective benefit, A and B would both need to stay silent.

The dominant strategy, however, is to optimize for individual gain and to defect. So the most likely end state, or the Nash Equilibrium, is that they reach a suboptimal outcome and both serve a longer time.

The payoff matrix for building products (figure 14) looks very similar to Prisoners' Dilemma. We could all choose to maximize individual gains and find local maxima (Uncontrolled Digital Pollution quadrant), or we could embrace the responsibility that comes with

FIGURE 14: Prisoner's Dilemma payoff matrix when building products

building products and maximize the collective benefit to society by finding the global maximum (Sustainable Growth quadrant).

The dominant strategy in the case of capitalism is to optimize profits for individual gain. In fact, the shareholder capitalism ideology demands it. In his hugely influential essay in 1970, Milton Friedman declared that the one and only responsibility of a business is to maximize profits. He considered straying outside this responsibility and thinking about social impact as socialism.[7] This ideology became popular, and Jack Welch, GE's CEO in 1981, popularized the shareholder primacy model in his speech where he said that the primary responsibility of a company was to its shareholders.[8] This ideology has led to an accepted dichotomy in business where we accept that you can do good *or* do well.

If we all optimize for profits while knowing that others are doing the same and rationalize our actions by saying, "If I don't build it, someone else will," we're heading toward the Nash Equilibrium in the Uncontrolled Digital Pollution quadrant. In this quadrant we maximize individual gains but generate a suboptimal situation for everyone in the long run.

The free-market ideology is often offered as a panacea: "If you trade off customers' well-being, they'll vote with their dollars." The belief is that markets are efficient and will resolve this problem. Unfortunately, the important underlying assumption of the free-market argument is that information is transparently available so users can make informed decisions. This fundamental assumption has been proven false.

In the case of dating platforms, for example, it wouldn't be obvious to Black women that the issue lies with the platforms and not with them. They wouldn't know that they are seeing disproportionately fewer messages—they may just feel unsuccessful in their online dating efforts. In the case of search results, if all the search results on the first page state something as fact, you're more likely to believe the information—it would seem corroborated by multiple sources. In the case of Purdue Pharma, patients trust doctors to prescribe the right medicine at the right dose for them. If doctors prescribe higher doses, patients assume that's what they need.

ESCAPING THE GRAVITY OF
A SUBOPTIMAL NASH EQUILIBRIUM

How do we avoid getting stuck in a suboptimal quadrant where businesses pursue short-term gains at the cost of societal well-being? How do we get business leaders to embrace responsible profitability? This is a question that regulators spend a lot of time thinking about. I interviewed Ravi Menon, managing director of the Monetary Authority of Singapore, Singapore's financial regulator and central bank, who said, "Regulations are important, but regulations alone aren't the answer—we can never be everywhere all the time and detect everything." Menon explained his framework of three *I*s to bring about the right behavior:

1. *Intimidation/Consequences:* In any society you need to deter bad behaviors by clarifying and enacting consequences when people (or organizations) do harm. This is where regulations come in.
2. *Incentives:* Incentives give you the economic rationale for doing the right thing because it aligns with one's self-interest. Incentives work better with human motivation than intimidation.
3. *Inspiration:* This taps into the intrinsic desire to do the right thing because we recognize the impact of our business on society.

Let's look at how we can apply each of these *I*s in the context of the tech industry.

Intimidation/Consequences

We've seen how regulations work to prevent uncontrolled environmental pollution. In 2014, BP reached a settlement of over $20 billion with the Department of Justice for its Deepwater Horizon oil spill, which pumped over 134 million gallons of oil into the Gulf of Mexico. The US attorney general at the time, Loretta Lynch, announced that the settlement was designed to not only compensate for damages but "let other companies know they are going to be responsible for the harm that occurs should accidents like this happen in the future."[9] Without regulations, the dominant strategy would be to recklessly pollute the environment because it's more profitable to build companies this way (at least in the short term).

The status quo with unabated digital pollution is unsustainable, and it's clear that we need regulations. However, regulations take a long time to be enacted. If you went back to London in the 1600s, you would find a coal-fired metropolis, where heavy smoke from the city's burning hearths and furnaces damaged buildings. Only during the Industrial Revolution in the mid-1800s, when respiratory diseases became the leading cause of death in the city, did people finally recognize how air pollution was affecting their quality of life. It took even longer to galvanize people into action. Only in 1956, over a century later, were laws with teeth finally enacted to significantly improve air quality in London.[10]

It took 300 years to legislate air pollution when its effects were visible to the naked eye. Digital pollution is more abstract, and we're still at step one and only just starting to recognize its effects on our society. While regulations can help us avoid the Uncontrolled Digital Pollution quadrant eventually, they may not help our generation (or even our children). Given the effects of digital pollution that we're already seeing in terms of destabilizing democracies, we cannot wait decades for laws with teeth to be enacted.

One problem regulators face is that with emerging technologies, the unintended consequences are not always clear until the technology is widespread. Further, if you regulate an emerging technology too early without fully understanding it, you may also curb the potential benefits. The result is that regulations will always play catch-up, and even when we have regulations in place, we cannot rely on regulations alone to curb digital pollution. Regulations must complement incentives and inspiration.

Incentives

When news about the environmental impact of a company or unethical business practices gets public attention, the damage to an organization's brand reputation serves as an incentive to consider not just shareholder interests but also societal or stakeholder interests.

In the absence of regulations in the tech industry, public shaming and the secondary effects of a drop in share prices serve a similar purpose as intimidation. Consumer advocacy and activism to raise awareness of unethical practices is invaluable. However, this is a negative incentive, and human nature is such that fear and punishment are not the best motivators to drive business leaders to take a proactive stance in trying to create a better world.

Further, when the next crisis comes along, consumer interest shifts to the next issue and stock prices typically recover. Each public scandal that featured Facebook marked a mild, temporary dip in Facebook's share price, but Facebook is still doing well financially and its stock price continues to soar.

By way of a positive incentive in the form of economic benefits to being ethical, research by UK's Institute of Business Ethics (IBE) shows that ethical companies (those that had codes of business ethics/conduct and abided by them) produced an above-average performance when measured against a similar group without codes.[11] One possible explanation for this may be that when values are lived, decision-making is more consistent at every level, which in turn increases employees' confidence and motivation.

The IBE study shows that a socially responsible approach can go hand in hand with profits—we've accepted a false choice with Friedman's ideology of shareholder primacy.

Inspiration

Studies show that the biggest motivator for humans is intrinsic.[12] While it seems idealistic to think that we have the intrinsic desire to do the right thing, one cause for optimism is that studies show that as humans, we're hardwired for collaboration. In looking at MRI scans of people playing Prisoner's Dilemma, researchers found that when the players cooperated, activity in the ventral striatum, the brain's reward center, would light up.[13] More importantly, they found that the reward center was more sensitive to the collective gains for both players, rather than to either player's individual gains.[14] Our ancestors survived through cooperation and as a result our neural mechanisms have evolved to give us gratification from attending to our collective well-being rather than maximizing individual benefit.

This desire for cooperation is manifested in our motivation. We yearn to find meaning and purpose in what we do and go to great lengths to believe that we're increasing our collective well-being through our work even when evidence indicates otherwise. Many people I've spoken to who work at Facebook don't feel that their work at the company is harming society. In fact, one employee said to me genuinely, "If I thought we were making the world worse off, I'd quit immediately." The employee is still at Facebook two years later.

This paradox is understandable because taking individual responsibility is difficult when the systems we work on are so complex. Each person typically works on a very small piece of the system and is most likely too far removed to see a causal link between the scope of that work and the harm to fellow humans. Further, when any one component on its own doesn't necessarily present an ethical issue or cause harm but the system does, it becomes harder to take individual responsibility.

In our desire to find meaning and purpose, we learn to compartmentalize work as a necessary means to earn money and use philanthropy to satisfy our desire to attend to our collective well-being. Philanthropy allows us to see ourselves as ethical and responsible by contributing toward making the world a little better.

Many well-known industrialists from the late 19th century took this approach of compartmentalizing their philanthropic efforts after amassing wealth from questionable business practices and were called robber barons. Andrew Carnegie, whose gifts enabled the construction of Carnegie Hall, the legendary New York City concert venue that opened in 1891, the Carnegie Institution for Science, Carnegie Mellon University, and the Carnegie Foundation, made his fortune as a steel magnate and ruthless industrialist.

In 1892, Carnegie Steel's main plant was the site of one of the most serious labor confrontations in history. The steel industry was doing well and the union asked for a wage increase, but the general manager, Henry Frick, whom Carnegie supported, counterproposed a wage decrease. When negotiations broke down, Frick proceeded to lock the workers out and bring in 300 security guards to protect the plant. The resulting scuffle between the striking workers and the guards left 10 people dead and many injured. The plant eventually resumed operations with nonunion workers but approximately 2,500 workers lost their jobs. Those who survived the cuts agreed to reduced wages and gruelling 12-hour shifts.[15]

Carnegie Steel increased income inequality by eroding workers' rights. While Andrew Carnegie gave away most of his wealth after he retired at the age of 65, his philanthropy supported the arts and elite institutions. It didn't improve inequality or workers' rights, the problems his work contributed to.

Data shows that this is not just a problem with Carnegie's approach to philanthropy but a wider issue. Statistics show that the United States is one of the most philanthropic nations, but inequality continues to rise—only a fifth of the money from large donors goes to the poor.

The reason behind this paradox is revealed by a 2013 research study that found wealthy Americans' preferences differ significantly from those of the general public on many important issues. The wealthy are much more favorable toward cutting social welfare programs, especially Social Security and healthcare. They are considerably less supportive of several jobs and income programs, including an above-poverty-level minimum wage.[16] As a result, their donations often go toward causes they find important and may not match the needs of the society at large. The robber baron strategy is not effective if we want to create a better world. We cannot compartmentalize doing well through business and doing good through philanthropy.

THE HIPPOCRATIC OATH OF PRODUCT

To effectively channel this intrinsic desire to maximize our collective well-being, we have to integrate responsibility into our business practices through the Hippocratic Oath of Product. There's growing awareness that we need to shift from a mindset of shareholder primacy to one of stakeholder capitalism. The World Economic Forum released the Davos Manifesto 2020, which explains the difference through its definition of a company as more than an economic unit generating wealth. "It fulfills human and societal aspirations as part of the broader social system. Performance must be measured not only on the return to shareholders, but also on how it achieves its environmental, social and good governance objectives."[17] To embrace the Hippocratic Oath of Product, we must shift our mindset from shareholder primacy to stakeholder capitalism.

More specifically, here are five things you can do to embrace the Hippocratic Oath of Product at every step of building your product:

1. *Vision:* Center your vision on your user. The template for the Radical Vision Statement helps you write your statement such that your vision is not about your aspirations for yourself or your company but is centered on the problem that you want to see solved for a group of people.

    While vision statements often describe financial goals— for example, "To change how people communicate and become a billion-dollar company in the process"—you'll notice that a Radical Vision Statement does not. Why? Imagine your doctor's vision statement included aspirations for billing: "To cure patients' ailments and build a practice of over $1 million a year." Would you expect the same level of care if her vision for her practice was about billing?

    In 1998, WorldCom stated its end goal as, "Our objective is to be the most profitable, single-source provider of communications services to customers around the world."[18] After an acquisition spree and an ensuing accounting scandal, WorldCom filed one of the largest bankruptcies in US history in 2002.[19]

    Your daily business needs, such as reaching revenue targets, are constantly beckoning you to the dark side. In Jedi terms, your vision must bring balance to the Force—your vision must counterbalance the pull from your profitability goals. If your vision is about becoming a billion-dollar company or about your billings, it becomes easy to lose sight of the change you wanted to create in the first place.

2. *Strategy:* Craft your RDCL strategy to align your business model with your users' needs. Take the example of insurance—when you make an insurance claim, it eats out of the insurer's profits. If you've ever claimed insurance, you have experienced firsthand that your insurer has every incentive to deny your claim. Lemonade Insurance developed a business model that aligns its incentives with its users'—the company makes money by taking a fixed fee from users' insurance premiums. What's unclaimed goes toward charity. By reimagining its product and business model, the company has aligned its incentives with users' needs.

3. *Prioritization:* Ensure that your values and ethical considerations affect your priorities and decision-making. When Enron became the center of one of the biggest accounting scandals of its time in 2001, it had a formal Enron code of ethics, a 64-page manual stating its ethical policies employees were expected to follow.[20]

   When the CFO at the time, Andrew Fastow, was engineering complex transactions to hide corporate losses and poorly performing assets, the board of directors realized that this was a violation of the code of ethics. So they decided to take action: they suspended the application of the code of ethics to Fastow while he was working on these transactions. Often company values are prominently displayed as conference room names. But they're ignored in the meetings within.

   Your company values are valued only if you show that they affect your priorities and decisions. You can use the vision-fit-versus-survival rubric to recognize when you're deviating from your purpose and plan course corrections.

4. *Execution and measurement:* Reevaluate the way you measure success. In the case of Lijjat, the organization doesn't measure success by revenues or whether it's dominating the pappadum market. It measures success by one metric: the number of women for whom Lijjat creates financial independence.

We often conflate product usage with success of the *product*. Instead, the success of the product should be defined by whether you achieved what you set out to achieve in the first place.

When designers at Facebook came up with the idea of the Like button, it was repeatedly proposed and shot down for two years, never passing Mark Zuckerberg's review. Ironically, his concern was that it would replace high-value interactions such as sharing and commenting with a simple click of the Like button. Going by the numbers, when the Like button was launched in 2009, it was a huge win.

Since then, the cocreators of the Like button, Leah Pearlman and Justin Rosenstein (who are no longer at Facebook), have expressed regret in their media interviews for creating spirals of distressing, addictive behavior through the iconic thumbs-up button.[21]

You can't always predict the unintended consequences of your products. This is why it's important to measure the success or failure of your product by whether it has achieved the impact that you intended. Embracing responsibility requires a mindset shift from viewing your product as a mechanism for maximizing financial metrics; when your product is an *improvable tool* to achieve the impact you want to have, you can course correct if real-world results don't match your desired impact.

5. *Culture:* Infuse a purpose beyond profit-making in your organizational culture.

"It doesn't happen through lip service," says Mike Rockwell in sharing an example from his role as executive vice president of products and technologies at Dolby. "You have to be willing to make decisions that illustrate what level you're optimizing at. We could optimize for profits or for the success of the human race. When we built 3D glasses at Dolby, our decisions communicated that we cared about our customer's comfort."

In 3D technology, you have to reduce cross-talk and ghosting between the left and right eye on the glasses. "Our solution just needed to be better than the competition's. But we went far beyond what we needed to because we cared about the customer's comfort." Through their product decisions, Rockwell and Dolby's leadership team communicated purpose and the organization's social norms and guidelines on user well-being.

We don't build our products with malicious intent. A lot of the collateral damage to society comes from the unintended consequences of our products. When we embed responsibility in our culture, anyone in our organization can recognize and call out outcomes and behavior that don't match the social norms and guidelines we define. This also requires a culture where there is psychological safety to speak up.

When we build products responsibly, we're keeping our focus on the user and the change we want to create for them. This doesn't mean we have to be altruistic—if we don't make a profit, we may not survive long enough to achieve our vision.

Radical Product Thinking gives you a repeatable methodology to build successful products while avoiding the product diseases that make good products go bad. In wielding the five elements of the RPT approach, you have a superpower that allows you to build vision-driven products that deeply affect people's lives. But with that superpower comes responsibility, and this chapter has given you practical steps so you can take the Hippocratic Oath of Product. You can choose to pursue profits responsibly and build products that bring about the change you envision to make the world just a little more like the one we want to live in.

KEY TAKEAWAYS

- In building a product, your role is much like that of a doctor. You're solving a problem for your users and it comes with the responsibility of their well-being.
- Prisoner's Dilemma helps illustrate the decision-making rationale of building products to maximize individual gain versus building responsibly.
- If everyone maximizes for individual gain, as a society we're heading toward a suboptimal outcome of unabated digital pollution.
- To avoid this outcome we need to consider a holistic approach that includes the three *I*s:
  - *Intimidation/Consequences:* Regulations to discourage bad behavior
  - *Incentives:* External motivation to encourage building responsibly
  - *Inspiration:* Awareness of how we affect society, tapping into our hardwired desire to maximize our collective well-being
- Compartmentalizing business as a mechanism to maximize profitability and philanthropy as a way of doing good isn't effective if we want to create a better world through our products.
- Taking the Hippocractic Oath of Product means baking ethics into each of the five elements of the RPT methodology (vision, strategy, prioritization, execution and measurement, and culture).

CONCLUSION
Radical Product Thinkers
Creating Change

As you build vision-driven products to bring about the change you want to see in the world, you can take inspiration from other Radical Product Thinkers around the world. This chapter offers examples of how RPT can be applied in different walks of life. You can create change in whatever way inspires you.

We'll start with the example of a Radical Product Thinker who is breaking through the dichotomy in an industry where profit seems like the sole purpose: finance. We'll then look at how each of us can apply RPT at any level and across an organization. Lastly, we'll stretch the thinking on product so that you can even think about the change you want to create through your personal life. Anything can be your product if it's your mechanism to bring about the change you envision in the world.

FINANCE AS A RADICAL PRODUCT

"It's not enough for finance to do no harm. Finance must be a force for good." I first heard Ravi Menon say this about finance at the Symposium on Asian Banking and Finance in 2019. Menon is the managing director of the Monetary Authority of Singapore (MAS), the central bank that issues currency, sets the monetary policy, and regulates banking, insurance, securities, and the financial sector in Singapore.

The idea that profitability and responsibility are mutually exclusive is more prevalent in the financial sector than in most other industries. After the 2008 financial crisis, where banks in the United States and Europe had to be bailed out using taxpayer money, even the idea of finance doing no harm seems like a stretch. The reckless pursuit of profit led to the worst recession since the Great Depression and roughly seven million Americans lost their homes. While Singaporean banks have generally fared much better in this regard, they too have recorded a few misdeeds. Could finance be a force for good?

Having lived in Singapore for two and a half years, I've repeatedly observed government agencies engineering change systematically. The RPT philosophy of envisioning change and translating it methodically from vision to execution has been embedded in Singapore's inception and its transformation from a poor, struggling island in the 1950s to an economic powerhouse. My optimism for finance as a force for good stems from seeing this history of product thinking in Singapore and hearing Menon's purpose-driven and methodical approach for the change he wants to bring about.

Menon shares his vision for finance by starting with the problem he sees in the sector: "Why do we have financial crisis after financial crisis? One reason is the difference between the financial industry and other sectors. When you build a product or a service, you need to make a profit, but you see that you're offering a benefit to society. For example, as a hairdresser, you care that you helped your customers look good—it makes you go the extra mile for your customer. But the majority of activities in finance, such as trading and derivatives, are purely about making a profit. You don't have a direct relationship with the customer and it's very impersonal." The further removed you are from helping a customer, the less you think about responsible profitability.

To make finance a force for good, Menon envisions that activities in the financial sector must be connected to a human-centered purpose. He gives the example of insurance and how MAS is helping infuse the human connection into this industry.

Having insurance is analogous to having shock absorbers in a car—it smoothes the ride when you encounter a bump in the road. Insurance that's widely available and inclusive would be a benefit to society.

Using data and machine learning to optimize profits without thinking about the human connection would break the model of insurance and create unintended consequences for society. The business model behind health insurance, for example, requires that a large number of people buy insurance but only a few get sick and claim insurance. But what if you could use machine learning to accurately predict who will claim insurance? You could maximize profits by excluding them, but in the process you would create a category of people who are uninsurable. Ironically, having imperfect knowledge is helpful if you want insurance to be inclusive.

"We're very worried about the fact that [having lots of data] can create an increasingly larger group of people who become uninsurable or their premiums will become extremely high," Menon explains. "But how do you make the argument that you must use less information in deciding premiums?" The algorithm may be making data-driven decisions, but this may still lead to outcomes that are not good for society by excluding parts of the population.

Menon's holistic strategy goes beyond regulations to manage the threat of digital pollution or unintended consequences for society from machine learning and algorithmic advances in finance.

To get organizations to embrace responsibility using the three *Is* (intimidation/consequences, incentives, ind Inspiration) MAS needed them to be more aware of what their models were doing. So when AI developers in Singapore reached out to MAS to share their concerns about how machine-learning models could impact society, MAS took the opportunity to facilitate an industry discussion.

In 2018, leaders in the financial industry, AI researchers, and MAS leadership cocreated a set of FEAT Principles (fairness, ethics, accountability, and transparency) that were publicly declared as an outcome from this discussion.[1] The FEAT Principles garnered attention around the world—it was the first time that an industry and a regulator cocreated guidelines for the responsible use of AI and data analytics.

"It's too early to create enforcement and supervision mechanisms around many of these evolving areas, and regulations will always lag behind innovation," Menon explains. "In the meanwhile, these publicly declared principles serve as a powerful reference for acceptable social norms as well as examples of behavior that will be looked down upon." Menon's strategy demonstrates a systematic approach to engineer change. To regulate the unintended consequences to society from innovation, he started by creating generally accepted social norms and awareness of the possible harm to society from irresponsible use of technology.

As part of shifting the financial sector toward a more human-centered approach, Menon believes that MAS too must be driven by empathy when interacting with the companies it regulates. One of the core tenets behind MAS's digital transformation initiative is "driven by empathy and centered on people."

In translating this human-centered approach into action, product teams at MAS use the RPT methodology to define a vision that's centered on users and the change they're setting out to create for them. In execution and measurement, teams measure the success of their digital products by whether they're creating the change they intended for their users.

There's also a conscious effort to embed the values of empathy and being centered on people in the organizational culture. For example, internal guidelines dictate that whenever possible, an MAS officer should not request a data submission from the industry just before leaving for a long weekend as this would likely mean that compliance officers at banks would have to work over the holiday to provide this data.

Menon is very clear that empathy for financial institutions doesn't mean loosening regulations or their enforcement: "Even if our answer is a 'No,' we can make the process of getting to that answer easier for the person on the other end. We can treat them as another human."

To be clear, growth in the financial sector and monetary KPIs are very important for MAS. A declining financial sector would have to focus on survival and make it harder for finance to be a force for good. Going back to the two-by-two of profit versus purpose (figure 11), MAS is pursuing growth and profits in the financial sector to support a human-centered purpose.

Menon takes a clear stance in favor of stakeholder capitalism and responsible profits over shareholder capitalism, where the sole responsibility of a business is to make profits: "Every business needs to define its larger purpose by how it's making the world a better place. Building the best product and maximizing shareholder value should still be subordinate to this larger purpose."

Menon extends this idea of purpose to the role of the individual: "In life, as it is in business, purpose is the ultimate compass. We have to ask ourselves why we are doing what we're doing." In our own small ways, each of us can make the world a better place through our business, our activities, and our expertise in a way that's compatible with making profits. This gets to the heart of Radical Product Thinking.

For Menon, the change he envisions is making finance a force for good in society. His work is his constantly improvable mechanism to bring about this change, a radical product.

EACH OF US CAN BUILD RADICAL PRODUCTS

Each of us can envision the change we want to bring about through our work, regardless of our role and place in the hierarchy. You don't have to be the leader of an organization to be a Radical Product Thinker. You can apply RPT at every level and across your organization to translate vision into execution. The story of the moon landing illustrates this approach.

On July 20, 1969, minutes before the lunar module *Eagle* was scheduled to touch down on the moon, dashboard alarms began to indicate an emergency. It warned the astronauts that the radar switch was in the wrong position for the moon landing. Buzz Aldrin realized his mistake and quickly fixed the error, but by then the radar had already bombarded the onboard computer with unnecessary data—the alarms were indicating that the in-flight computer wasn't keeping up with the calculations required of it. Mission Control and the astronauts had to make a go/no-go decision on the landing.

President John F. Kennedy was the leader at the helm who had the audacious vision of putting a man on the moon. But the reason the *Apollo 11* mission was a success and not a disaster was because of the work of Margaret Hamilton—a programmer who had a clear vision for how software should be engineered when lives were at stake.

With three minutes left until landing, it was clear that the in-flight software had recovered and was continuing its tasks. Hamilton, who was in charge of the onboard flight software, had architected the system so that in the event of an overload, the onboard computer would ignore all unnecessary tasks and focus only on a prioritized list that was essential for landing. Mission Control was able to give the astronauts the green light, and we all know what followed: the landing was a success, Neil Armstrong walked on the moon, and the United States achieved its "giant leap for mankind."

Even in this day and age, this would be considered remarkably good software engineering. But at the time, no schools taught software engineering and the team was pioneering its work, learning on the job. So how did Hamilton design this in the '60s, when software wasn't even recognized as a field in engineering? Hamilton's answer reflects a vision-driven approach: she had a clear picture of the end state she wanted to create through her product (the in-flight software). "Our software had to be man-rated, which meant lives were at stake. It had to work the first time. Not only did the software itself have to be ultrareliable, but the software needed to be able to detect an error and recover from it in real time," she says. Hamilton had translated NASA's vision (putting a man on the moon) into her vision for her work (building software that's reliable enough to recover from any possible error in the process of putting a man on the moon).

Hamilton pioneered the field of software engineering from that vision. "Having this kind of responsibility [for the astronauts' lives] resulted in our creating a 'field' since there was no school at the time to learn 'software engineering.' We were always looking for new ways to prevent errors. This necessitated our creating methods, standards, rules, and tools for developing the flight software. When answers could not be found, we had to invent them as we went along," she explains.

When you're higher up in the organization, you may not always have visibility or an understanding of the details to make the right decisions at a micro level—you need all individuals to translate the organization's vision into their own work. Hamilton describes it as a paradigm where "vision had no boundaries." All individuals had to have a vision for how their work would help achieve the goal of putting a man on the moon.

When we take a vision-driven approach to building products, we think holistically about the impact of our work. For example, if you're a vision-driven software developer, you don't find satisfaction just in making your code work but in whether the system works to achieve your shared goal. Hamilton's vision-driven approach meant that she didn't view her responsibility as limited to programming; instead, her solutions for reliability often touched every aspect of the system design—from hardware to mission structure to astronauts' actions. This was novel thinking at NASA at the time and, occasionally, this focus on reliability was deemed more than what was necessary for a space mission.

On one occasion, Hamilton was working in the lab over the weekend when her daughter, Lauren, accidentally crashed the simulation through a series of keystrokes while "playing astronaut." It turned out she had inadvertently selected the launch code (P01) and then selected the prelaunch program (P00). Hamilton realized that if her daughter could crash the system by doing that, an astronaut could too and wanted to add error checking to prevent this issue. But NASA rejected this idea as unnecessary since astronauts were trained to be perfect and wouldn't make such mistakes.

This view changed soon after when on Christmas Day, the *Apollo 8* mission was midway into its mission and ran into trouble. The software had crashed and wiped all the navigational data—without it the astronauts were adrift in space without a path home. Astronaut Jim Lovell had run into "the Lauren problem"—he had accidentally selected P01 midflight and later P00. Hamilton and the team got the system back up by figuring out how to reupload the navigational data from Houston.[2] For NASA, this event demonstrated the importance of Hamilton's vision-driven approach that traversed the boundaries of software, and they gave Hamilton carte blanche to make her error detection and recovery code standard across all Apollo software.

When I spoke with Hamilton about the need for a vision-driven approach when we build products, she agreed and contrasted her approach against the approach Boeing took in building the 737 MAX. Whereas Hamilton's vision led her to prevent errors in any part of the system, the 737 MAX design relies on fixing errors: to overcome the aerodynamic instability caused by the hardware design, the plane relies on the MCAS software, which, in turn, relies on the pilots to overcome the errors and maneuver the plane in case of a critical failure in the software. "I'd never fly on a 737 MAX, although it's been recertified by the FAA," Hamilton concludes.

Hamilton pioneered the concept of defensive coding, led by the vision that software should prevent errors and recover from them if they do occur.[3] NASA recognized her work with the Space Act Award in 2003, and more recently she was awarded the Presidential Medal of Freedom in 2016. Hamilton's vision, and the resulting technique that saved the moon landing, were essential to achieving President Kennedy's vision of putting a man on the moon. We need Radical Product Thinkers who can translate a vision into action at every level and across our organization.

BUILDING RADICAL PRODUCTS
IN OUR PERSONAL LIVES

Beyond the confines of your work environment, you can also apply Radical Product Thinking in your everyday life. You can engineer change by being purposeful in your actions whether through volunteering in the community or through activism to make the world a little more like the one you'd want to live in.

This is what 15-year-old Claudette Colvin did on March 2, 1955. Colvin and her friends were on a bus in Montgomery, Alabama, returning home from school that day. They were sitting toward the back of the bus, as required by segregation rules. But after a few stops as the bus filled up, a white woman was left standing and the bus driver instructed Colvin and her friends to give up their seats for the young woman.

While Colvin's friends got up reluctantly, she refused. Colvin explains that she would have given up her seat for an elderly person, but this was a young woman. The driver threatened to call the police, but she didn't budge. Colvin was arrested that day for defying the bus segregation laws in Alabama.

I asked Colvin how she stood up to authority when she wasn't even an adult. "When I refused to get up, it wasn't a planned protest. I just wanted the people on the bus to know that what they were doing was wrong. They needed to know that segregation was unfair and that I was being treated unjustly."

Colvin was just 15 years old, but she knew that the world she wanted to live in was one where everyone was equal. Colvin was 79 when I spoke to her in 2018 and sounded a little tired at the beginning of our conversation, but as she started talking about the world she wanted to see, her voice lit up: "Everyone who's African American had to prove that they were someone and not inferior. I just wanted access to a better life, a better education. I wanted a world where we all had the same American Dream, where we could live the same American Dream as the white people. I was tired of adults complaining about how badly they were treated and not doing anything about it."

Colvin knew about the risks of being arrested: there was the risk of police brutality while under arrest, and even after her release there was the risk of retaliation by the KKK against her whole family—yet she stayed in her seat because she had a vision for the world she wanted to live in. She envisioned a world where we could all share the same American Dream.

Two weeks after her arrest, Rosa Parks called her parents and invited Colvin to speak to the youth group Parks was leading. Colvin became secretary of the youth council of the NAACP and met with Rosa Parks regularly. Nine months after Colvin was arrested, Parks defied the segregation laws in the same way and was arrested. Rosa Parks became the icon of the civil rights movement and her case rallied the community.

While Colvin's spontaneous protest of refusing to give up her seat was remarkably brave, her follow-through on her actions is even more admirable as she pursued change very deliberately. Colvin was a plaintiff and key witness with a fiery testimony in *Browder v. Gayle*, a Supreme Court case that led to the landmark ruling making segregation on buses illegal.[4] There was immense pressure to back out of the lawsuit. In fact, the lawsuit lists four plaintiffs (Aurelia Browder, Susie McDonald, Claudette Colvin, and Mary Louise Smith) because the fifth plaintiff, Jeanetta Reese, was intimidated into withdrawing from the lawsuit. Accepting the status quo would have been an easier path, but Colvin had a clear sense of purpose in fighting the injustice.

Despite Colvin's contribution to the civil rights movement, she was largely forgotten by history. Many articles on the internet suggest that she was passed over as the icon for the civil rights movement because she was pregnant at the time of her arrest—but this is historically inaccurate. Colvin's purpose-driven approach is evident when she explains matter-of-factly why it made sense to choose Rosa Parks as the icon instead of her. "They needed someone who would be accepted by everyone, blacks and whites alike. Mrs. Parks was lighter skinned. Fairer people were viewed as having some European blood. They were treated better by both whites and blacks. She also came from a middle-class background." Colvin lived in the poor part of the neighborhood. Colvin was pursuing change deliberately and she recognized that she had created a spark, but if she wanted to grow it into a fire, someone like Rosa Parks (who would be accepted by the masses) needed to carry the torch.

Colvin says she has no regrets for taking a stand despite the lack of recognition: "I worked hard and I feel like I've gotten to see the fruit of my labor through my grandchildren. I lost one son, but my other son has done really well and has a PhD in business. I have five grandchildren and five great-grandchildren. Fortunately, none of them have gotten caught in the system.

"And I got to see Barack Obama elected president."

Whether you work in a nonprofit, a government organization, research, a high tech startup, freelancing, or activism, you have a product. Any of these could be your improvable mechanism to create change.

In building your product, instead of iterating in the pure pursuit of financial KPIs, you can take the purpose-driven approach of Radical Product Thinking. RPT gives you a methodology to systematically build successful products while avoiding the common product diseases that get in the way by following these five steps:

1. Create a compelling vision of the change you want to bring about.
2. Craft a strategy to give you an actionable plan.
3. Prioritize so that your vision features in your everyday decision making.
4. Measure what matters to know if you're making progress toward your vision.
5. Embed your purpose in your organizational culture.

The RPT approach also helps you embrace the responsibility that comes with building successful products that impact people's lives. You can bake your human-centered purpose into every step as you build your products.

Over the last 50 years, it has been ingrained in us that the role of *business (and therefore* of products) is the pursuit of profit. We had accepted the idea that we could either build successful products or engage in philanthropy to make the world a better place. This ideology was reflected in how we were building products—we often overrelied on iteration to optimize for financial metrics. But in the process, our products have caught diseases and often inflicted collateral damage to society. Our approach to date has been like riding on a galloping horse—it gives you the thrill of moving fast even if your horse may be going in the wrong direction. We're seeing that this is no longer sustainable.

Radical Product Thinking helps you grab hold of the reins to systematically bring about the change you envision in the world, big or small, through your activities and your expertise. Radical Product Thinking helps you innovate smarter so you can build vision-driven products that do good and do well.

ACKNOWLEDGMENTS

want to start by thanking you, the Radical Product Thinker, for your drive to create vision-driven change. You're already spending time in the Investing in the Vision quadrant by choosing to read this book.

I'm deeply grateful to Geordie Kaytes and Nidhi Aggarwal—the idea of writing a book started from our collaboration, which remains one of the most memorable experiences in my career. As we cocreated the product diseases and the tools for vision, strategy, prioritization, and execution and measurement, we had help from many of you who were early adopters. You gave us feedback that refined the tool kit. We couldn't have created RPT without you!

Even with a powerful methodology, breaking into the publishing world, it turns out, is incredibly difficult. I'd like to thank Dan Ariely for his advice and making introductions when I started this book project. My break came through a chain of introductions that started with John Conway and included Jerry Tarde, Farley Chase, and Leah Spiro. I'm grateful to each of them for eventually leading me to Will Weisser.

I'm forever indebted to Will Weisser for his unwavering support in helping me find the right publisher. Will recognized Radical Product Thinking as a big idea, even in its unpolished form, and reminded me of it when I needed to hear it most.

I'm also grateful to Radical Product Thinkers around the world who egged me on to write this book. Many of you reached out over email or on LinkedIn to share how this methodology has helped you. These stories never get old, and I'm always grateful that you take the time to share them. Thank you!

A big thank-you to my editor, Anna Leinberger, who helped me avoid Strategic Swelling. The fact that you finished reading the book to get to the acknowledgments section is in no small part because of her. I'd also like to thank the team at Berrett-Koehler for taking on this project. I'm grateful to have found a publisher that cares about making the world a better place.

This book was driven by a clear vision, but the version you just read was the result of many iterations. A sincere thanks to Sharon Goldinger and the team at PeopleSpeak, Pamela Gordon, Britt Bravo, Buddy Blattner, Jennifer Joyce, Tim Maiden, Owen Johnson, Lucy Lubashev, Verena Hehl, and David Schleifer for your feedback along the way. I'm also grateful to David Schleifer for showing me what it meant to be vision-driven early in my career.

One of the most rewarding aspects of writing this book was the people I had a chance to interview. My sincere thanks to Ravi Menon for setting aside time on a weekend to share profound insights and reflections on how business can be a force for good—I am over-whelmed by your humility and generosity.

Learning about Lijjat's story was incredibly inspiring, and I'd like to thank Swati Paradkar for taking the time to help me share her story. I'm grateful to Margaret Hamilton and Claudette Colvin for deeply enriching conversations akin to thirst-quenchers for the soul. Beyond my gratitude alone, a whole generation is forever indebted to Claudette Colvin for the change she brought about during the civil rights movement and the sacrifices it required on her part.

I'd also like to thank the many Radical Product Thinkers who took the time to share their thoughts in my interviews with them: Bruce McCarthy, Bruno Tonelli, Yogesh Sharma, Sharif Mansour, Jeremy Kriegel, Jana Gombitova, Agnes Szeberenyi, Leala Abbot, Anne Griffin, Andy Ellis, Anthony Philippakis, Mukund Gopalakrishnan,

Brian Croft, Richard Kasperowski, Søren Fuhr, Cindy Beyer, Doug Shultz, David Minarsch, Martin Delius, Mike Rockwell, Sandra Bermudez, Artug Acar, and Phil Leacock. May-Li Khoe, thanks for our therapeutic discussions about the tech industry. Thanks to Paul Haun and Yarrow Thorne for your openness in allowing me to share our work together. I'm forever indebted to Antonio Pagano and Nicole Escobar from Wawandco for your support and creativity with the website.

This book was also profoundly shaped by my 2.5 years in Singapore. My work at the Monetary Authority of Singapore was a large part of it and remains one of the most satisfying experiences of my career and one that I've learned a lot from. I'm especially grateful to Carolyn Neo and the PebbleRoad team including Vasu Kolla and Maish Nichani for bringing me into MAS. A big thanks to Der Jiun Chia, Jacqueline Loh, Tuang Lee Lim, Cindy Mok, Keng Yi Lee, Jeremy Hor, and all my colleagues at MAS—I'm deeply inspired by your openness in embracing new ideas.

Finally, I'd like to thank my family. To my parents, I'm grateful for the biggest gift you could give me: unconditional love. You raised me to be persistent and to believe that I could change the world without feeling like I had to. To my brother for looking up to me as we were growing up—it made me want to live up to it.

To my kids, Arya and Rishi, thank you for being the bubbles in my life and for being my number one supporters—when I signed my publishing deal, for days you both went around exclaiming how excited you were for me. Thank you for reminding me to savor each victory before chasing the next.

To my husband, Daniele De Francesco, thank you for being my best friend and partner. I'm grateful for your love, understanding, and support as my every passion becomes an obsession; this book has proven to be no exception. We have a running joke at our dinner table that I'm the salmon swimming up the never-ending waterfall. You give me perspective. And I can tell you the view from here is so much better because you're by my side.

NOTES

INTRODUCTION

1. David Rowell, "Did Boeing Secretly 'Bet the Company' Yet Again on an Airline Project?" *Travel Insider*, July 18, 2019, http://blog.thetravelinsider.info /2019/07/did-boeing-secretly-bet-the-company-yet-again-on-an-airline-project.html.

2. *Seattle Times* business staff, "Timeline: A Brief History of the Boeing 737 MAX," *Seattle Times*, updated June 21, 2019, http://www.seattletimes.com /business/boeing-aerospace/timeline-brief-history-boeing-737-max/.

3. Boeing Company, *2018 Annual Report*, March 2019, http://s2.q4cdn .com/661678649/files/doc_financials/annual/2019/Boeing-2018AR-Final.pdf.

4. Yoel Minkoff, "Spotlight on Boeing Buybacks amid Latest Crisis," *Seeking Alpha*, March 19, 2020, http://seekingalpha.com/news/3553310-spotlight-on -boeing-buybacks-amid-latest-crisis.

5. Rachelle C. Sampson and Yuan Shi, "Are U.S. Firms Becoming More Short Term Oriented? Evidence of Shifting Firm Time Horizons from Implied Discount Rates, 1980–2013," *Strategic Management Journal* (March 26, 2020), https://doi.org/10.1002/smj.3158.

6. Clyde Prestowitz, *The Betrayal of American Prosperity: Free Market Delusions, America's Decline, and How We Must Compete in the Post-Dollar Era* (New York: Free Press, 2010).

7. Brian R. Cheffins, *The Public Company Transformed* (New York: Oxford University Press, 2019).

8. Tim Smart, "Ge's Money Machine," *Bloomberg*, March 7, 1993, http://www.bloomberg.com/news/articles/1993-03-07/ges-money-machine.

9. Nick Bilton, "All Is Fair in Love and Twitter," *New York Times*, October 9, 2013, http://www.nytimes.com/2013/10/13/magazine/all-is-fair-in-love-and -twitter.html.

CHAPTER 1

1. "Sandy Munro's Tesla Deep Dive—Autoline After Hours 447," *Autoline After Hours*, Autoline Network, streamed live January 3, 2019, http://www.youtube.com/watch?v=aVnRQRdePp4.

2. Mark Kane, "Tesla Model 3 Outsold Premium Competitors by 100,000 Since 2018," *InsideEVs*, June 10, 2019, http://insideevs.com/news/353847/tesla-model-3-outsold-premium-competitors/.

3. Chris Paine, *Who Killed the Electric Car?* (United States: Plinyminor, 2006), film.

4. Ralph Gomory and Richard Sylla, "The American Corporation," *Daedalus* 142, no.2 (Spring 2013): 102–118, https://doi.org/10.1162/daed_a_00207.

5. Lewis Carroll, *Alice's Adventures in Wonderland* (1865; New York: Dover, 1993), 41.

6. *Oxford English Dictionary*, s.v., "radical," accessed April 3, 2021, https://www.lexico.com/en/definition/radical.

7. *Singapore Free Press*, July 21, 1854.

8. "Transcript of a Press Conference Given by the Prime Minister of Singapore, Mr. Lee Kuan Yew, at the Broadcasting House, Singapore, at 1200 Hours on Monday 9th August, 1965," National Archives of Singapore, August 9, 1965, https://www.nas.gov.sg/archivesonline/data/pdfdoc/lky19650809b.pdf.

9. "Prime Minister's Press Conference Held on 26th August, 1965, at City Hall," National Archives of Singapore, August 26, 1965, http://www.nas.gov.sg/archivesonline/data/pdfdoc/lky19650826.pdf.

10. "Excerpts from an Interview with Lee Kuan Yew," *New York Times*, August 29, 2007, http://www.nytimes.com/2007/08/29/world/asia/29iht-lee-excerpts.html.

11. Chua Mui Hoong and Rachel Chang, "Did Mr Lee Kuan Yew Create a Singapore in His Own Image?" *Straits Times*, March 24, 2015, http://www.straitstimes.com/singapore/did-mr-lee-kuan-yew-create-a-singapore-in-his-own-image; and "Singapore Citizen's Passport Cancelled, Investigated for Possible Offences for Breaching Stay-Home Notice Requirements," Immigration & Checkpoints Authority, March 29, 2020, http://www.ica.gov.sg/news-and-publications/media-releases/media-release/singapore-citizen-s-passport-cancelled-investigated-for-possible-offences-for-breaching-stay-home-notice-requirements.

12. "Excerpts from an Interview."

13. Derek Wong, "Singapore Public Transport System Tops Global List," *Straits Times*, August 23, 2018, http://www.straitstimes.com/singapore/transport/spore-public-transport-system-tops-global-list.

14. "Prime Minister's Press Conference Held on 26th August, 1965."

15. "MOM's Vision, Mission and Values," Ministry of Manpower, Government of Singapore, last updated February 21, 2020, www.mom.gov.sg/about-us/vision-mission-and-values.

CHAPTER 2

1. Sahil Lavingia, "Reflecting on My Failure to Build a Billion-Dollar Company," *Marker*, February 7, 2019, http://medium.com/s/story/reflecting-on-my-failure-to-build-a-billion-dollar-company-b0c31d7db0e7.

2. Lizette Chapman, "Beepi Raising 'Monster Round' to Scale Used-Car Marketplace," *Wall Street Journal*, May 29, 2015, http://blogs.wsj.com/venturecapital/2015/05/29/beepi-raising-monster-round-to-scale-used-car-marketplace/.

3. Mary Ellen Biery, "The Big Impact of Small Businesses: 9 Amazing Facts," *Forbes*, October 22 2017, http://www.forbes.com/sites/sageworks/2017/10/22/the-big-impact-of-small-businesses-9-amazing-facts/.

4. Robert Longley, "How Small Business Drives U.S. Economy," ThoughtCo, updated January 2, 2020, http://www.thoughtco.com/how-small-business-drives-economy-3321945.

5. Jeffrey S. Passel and D'Vera Cohn, "Immigration Projected to Drive Growth in U.S. Working-Age Population through at least 2035," Pew Research Center, March 8, 2020, http://www.pewresearch.org/fact-tank/2017/03/08/immigration-projected-to-drive-growth-in-u-s-working-age-population-through-at-least-2035/.

6. US Census Bureau, "Older People Projected to Outnumber Children for the First Time in U.S. History," release no. CB18-41, last revised October 8, 2019, http://www.census.gov/newsroom/press-releases/2018/cb18-41-population-projections.html.

7. Clayton M. Christensen, *The Innovator's Dilemma: When New Technologies Cause Great Firms to Fail* (Boston: Harvard Business Review Press, 2016).

8. Associated Press, "Mary Gates, 64, Helped Her Son Start Microsoft," *New York Times*, June 11, 1994, https://www.nytimes.com/1994/06/11/obituaries/mary-gates-64-helped-her-son-start-microsoft.html; and Alex Planes, "How IBM Created the Future of the PC—and Almost Destroyed Its Own," Motley Fool, August 12, 2013, http://www.fool.com/investing/general/2013/08/12/how-ibm-created-the-future-of-the-pc-and-almost-de.aspx.

9. James Wallace and Jim Erickson, *Hard Drive: Bill Gates and the Making of the Microsoft Empire* (Chichester, UK: Wiley, 1993), http://www.e-reading.club/bookreader.php/1020153Wallace_-_Hard_Drive_Bill_Gates_and_the_Making_of_the_Microsoft_Empire.html.

10. Chethan Sathya, "Why Would Hospitals Forbid Physicians and Nurses from Wearing Masks?" *Scientific American*, March 26, 2020, http://blogs.scientific american.com/observations/why-would-hospitals-forbid-physicians-and-nurses -from-wearing-masks/.

CHAPTER 3

1. Shannon Schuyler and Abigail Brennan, *Putting Purpose to Work: A Study of Purpose in the Workplace*, PwC, June 2016, http://www.pwc.com/us/en /purpose-workplace-study.html; and Aaron Hurst et al., *Purpose at Work: 2016 Workforce Purpose Index*, LinkedIn and Imperative, 2016, https://cdn.imperative. com/media/public/Global_Purpose_Index_2016.pdf.

2. Josh Linkner, *The Road to Reinvention: How to Drive Disruption and Accelerate Transformation* (San Francisco, Jossey-Bass, 2014).

3. Jeffrey H. Dyer, Hall Gregersen, and Clayton M. Christensen, "The Innovator's DNA," *Harvard Business Review*, December 2009, http://hbr.org/2009/12 /the-innovators-dna.

CHAPTER 4

1.   Abhijit V. Banerjee and Esther Duflo, *Poor Economics: Barefoot Hedge-Fund Managers, DIY Doctors and the Surprising Truth about Life on Less Than $1 a Day* (London: Penguin, 2012).

2. Muhammad Yunus, "Sacrificing Microcredit for Megaprofits," *New York Times*, January 14, 2011, http://www.nytimes.com/2011/01/15/opinion/15yunus .html.

3. Lydia Polgreen and Vikas Bajaj, "India Microcredit Faces Collapse from Defaults," *New York Times*, November 17, 2010, http://www.nytimes.com/2010 /11/18/world/asia/18micro.html.

4. Ev Williams, "Our Approach to Member-Only Content," *3 Min Read* (blog), Medium, March 22, 2017, http://blog.medium.com/our-approach-to -member-only-content-cfce188261d1.

5. Laura Hazard Owen, (March 25, 2019). "The Long, Complicated, and Extremely Frustrating History of Medium, 2012–Present," Nieman Lab, March 25, 2019, http://www.niemanlab.org/2019/03/the-long-complicated-and-extremely -frustrating-history-of-medium-2012-present/.

6. Klaus Klemp and Keiko Ueki-Polet, eds., *Less and More: The Design Ethos of Dieter Rams* (Berlin: Die Gestalten Verlag, 2011); and Sophie Lovell, *The Work of Dieter Rams: As Little Design as Possible* (London: Phaidon, 2011).

7. Kate Moran, "The Aesthetic-Usability Effect," Nielsen Norman Group, January 29, 2017, http://www.nngroup.com/articles/aesthetic-usability-effect/.

8. Kate Moran, "The Impact of Tone of Voice on Users' Brand Perception," Nielsen Norman Group, August 7, 2016, http://www.nngroup.com/articles/tone-voice-users/.

9. For further reading on the subject of eliciting emotional reactions through design, check out Don Norman's *Emotional Design* and Aarron Walter's *Designing for Emotion*.

10. Netflix Inc., Mailing and response envelope, US Patent US6966484B2, filed September 16, 2002, and issued November 22, 2005.

11. Sam Levin, "Squeezed Out: Widely Mocked Startup Juicero Is Shutting Down," *Guardian*, September 1, 2017, http://www.theguardian.com/technology/2017/sep/01/juicero-silicon-valley-shutting-down.

CHAPTER 5

1. Nathaniel Koloc, "Let Employees Choose When, Where, and How to Work," *Harvard Business Review*, November 10, 2014, http://hbr.org/2014/11/let-employees-choose-when-where-and-how-to-work; and LRN, *The How Report: A Global Empirical Analysis of How Governance, Culture, and Leadership Impact Performance*, 2014, https://howmetrics.lrn.com.

CHAPTER 6

1. Remember that your measurements may also be qualitative and you may have to continue to interview users or observe them to understand where you can make continuous improvements.

2. Lisa D. Ordóñez et al., "Goals Gone Wild: The Systematic Side Effects of Overprescribing Goal Setting," *Academy of Management Perspectives* 23, no. 1 (2009): 6–16, http://doi.org/10.5465/amp.2009.37007999.

3. Christopher Earley, Terry Connolly, and Göran Ekegren, "Goals, Strategy Development, and Task Performance: Some Limits on the Efficacy of Goal Setting," *Journal of Applied Psychology* 74 (1989): 24–33.

4. Barry M. Staw and Richard D. Boettger, "Task Revision: A Neglected Form of Work Performance," *Academy of Management Journal* 33, no. 3 (1990): 534–559, www.jstor.org/stable/256580.

5. Ordóñez et al., "Goals Gone Wild," 6–16.

6. Maurice E. Schweitzer, Lisa Ordóñez, and Bambi Douma, "Goal Setting as a Motivator of Unethical Behavior," *Academy of Management Journal* 47, no. 3 (2004): 422–432.

7. Roger Lowenstein, "How Lucent Lost It," *MIT Technology Review*, February 1, 2005, http://www.technologyreview.com/2005/02/01/231676 /how-lucent-lost-it/.

8. Jack Kelly, "Wells Fargo Forced to Pay $3 Billion for the Bank's Fake Account Scandal," *Forbes*, February 24, 2020, http://www.forbes.com/sites /jackkelly/2020/02/24/wells-fargo-forced-to-pay-3-billion-for-the-banks-fake -account-scandal.

9. Edwin A. Locke and Gary P. Latham, *A Theory of Goal Setting and Task Performance* (Englewood Cliffs, NJ: Prentice Hall, 1990).

10. Evan I. Schwartz, "Laszlo Bock: Divorce Compensation from OKRs: Using OKRs to Power Growth, Engagement, and Diversity," *What Matters*, December 28, 2018, http://www.whatmatters.com/articles/laszlo-bock-divorce -compensation-from-okrs/.

11. Johanna Bolin Tingvall, "Why Individual OKRs Don't Work for Us," *Spotify HR Blog*, August 15, 2016, http://hrblog.spotify.com/2016/08/15 /our-beliefs/.

CHAPTER 7

1. Ben Wigert, "Employee Burnout: The Biggest Myth," Gallup, March 13, 2020, http://www.gallup.com/workplace/288539/employee-burnout-biggest -myth.aspx.

2. Daniel Pink, *Drive: The Surprising Truth about What Motivates Us* (Edinburgh: Canongate, 2018).

3. Anna Wiener, *Uncanny Valley* (London: HarperCollins UK, 2021).

4. Gallup Inc., "How to Prevent Employee Burnout," Gallup.com, September 11, 2020, http://www.gallup.com/workplace/313160/preventing-and-dealing -with-employee-burnout.aspx.

5. Margaret Heffernan, "Forget the Pecking Order at Work," TED, May 2015, http://www.ted.com/talks/margaret_heffernan_why_it_s_time_to _forget_the_pecking_order_at_work; and David Sloan Wilson, "When the Strong Outbreed the Weak: An Interview with William Muir," *This View of Life*, July 22, 2016, https://thisviewoflife.com/when-the-strong-outbreed-the-weak-an -interview-with-william-muir/.

6. Anita Williams Woolley et al., "Evidence for a Collective Intelligence Factor in the Performance of Human Groups," *Science* 330, no. 686 (2010): 686–688.

7. Maria Nokkonen, "Make Mental Strength Your Strongest Skill—the All Blacks Way," GamePlan A, March 1, 2017, http://www.gameplan-a.com/2017/03 /make-mental-strength-your-strongest-skill/.

8. Vivian Hunt, Dennis Layton, and Sara Prince, "Why Diversity Matters," McKinsey & Company, January 1, 2015, http://www.mckinsey.com /business-functions/organization/our-insights/why-diversity-matters.

9. Monica Anderson, "Black STEM Employees Perceive a Range of Race-Related Slights and Inequities at Work," Pew Research Center, January 10, 2018, http://www.pewresearch.org/fact-tank/2018/01/10/black-stem-employees -perceive-a-range-of-race-related-slights-and-inequities-at-work/.

10. Christian E. Weller, "African Americans Face Systematic Obstacles to Getting Good Jobs," Center for American Progress, December 5, 2019, http: //www.americanprogress.org/issues/economy/reports/2019/12/05/478150 /african-americans-face-systematic-obstacles-getting-good-jobs/.

11. Anderson, "Black STEM Employees."

12. Amy Edmondson, "Psychological Safety and Learning Behavior in Work Teams," *Administrative Science Quarterly* 44, no. 2 (June 1999): 350–383.

13. Amy C. Edmondson, "Managing the Risk of Learning: Psychological Safety in Work Teams," in *International Handbook of Organizational Teamwork and Cooperative Working*, eds. Michael West, Dean Tjasvold, and Ken Smith (Chichester, UK: Wiley, 2003), 255–275, https://www.hbs.edu/faculty /Publication%20Files/02-062_0b5726a8-443d-4629-9e75-736679b870fc.pdf.

14. Kim Scott, *Radical Candor: Be a Kick-Ass Boss without Losing Your Humanity* (New York: St. Martin's, 2019).

CHAPTER 8

1. Tim Bray, "Bye, Amazon," *Ongoing by Tim Bray* (blog), April 29, 2020, http://www.tbray.org/ongoing/When/202x/2020/04/29/Leaving-Amazon.

2. See http://www.techforgood.global.

3. David Autor and Anna Salomons, "Is Automation Labor Share-Displacing? Productivity Growth, Employment, and the Labor Share," *Brookings Papers on Economic Activity* 2018, no. 1 (Spring 2018): 1–87, http://doi.org/10.1353/eca.2018.0000.

4. Nick Yee, "7 Things We Learned about Primary Gaming Motivations from Over 250,000 Gamers," Quantic Foundry, December 15, 2016, http:// quanticfoundry.com/2016/12/15/primary-motivations/.

5. Prodigy Game, "What Is Prodigy Math Game?" Vimeo, posted December 17, 2015, https://vimeo.com/149299234.

6. Prodigy Education, "Prodigy Memberships," YouTube video, posted August 20, 2018, https://youtu.be/GHiqNI-_OT8.

7. Arielle Pardes, "This Dating App Exposes the Monstrous Bias of Algorithms," *Wired*, May 25, 2019, http://www.wired.com/story/monster-match-dating-app/.

8. Will Knight, "The Apple Card Didn't 'See' Gender—and That's the Problem," *Wired*, November 19, 2019, http://www.wired.com/story/the -apple-card-didnt-see-genderand-thats-the-problem/.

9. Julia Carpenter, "Google's Algorithm Shows Prestigious Job Ads to Men, but Not to Women. Here's Why That Should Worry You," *Washington Post*, July 6, 2015, http://www.washingtonpost.com/news/the-intersect/wp/2015/07/06 /googles-algorithm-shows-prestigious-job-ads-to-men-but-not-to-women-heres -why-that-should-worry-you/.

10. Rebecca Heilweil, "Artificial Intelligence Will Help Determine If You Get Your Next Job," *Vox*, December 12, 2019, http://www.vox.com/recode/2019/12 /12/20993665/artificial-intelligence-ai-job-screen.

11. Karen Hao, "AI Is Sending People to Jail—and Getting It Wrong," *MIT Technology Review*, January 21, 2019, http://www.technologyreview.com /2019/01/21/137783/algorithms-criminal-justice-ai/.

12. Cade Metz and Daisuke Wakabayashi, "Google Researcher Says She Was Fired over Paper Highlighting Bias in A.I.," *New York Times*, December 3, 2020, https://www.nytimes.com/2020/12/03/technology/google-researcher-timnit -gebru.html.

13. Kevin Kelleher, "Gilded Age 2.0: U.S. Income Inequality Increases to Pre–Great Depression Levels," *Fortune*, February 13, 2019, http://fortune.com /2019/02/13/us-income-inequality-bad-great-depression/.

14. Alexia Fernández Campbell, "The Recession Hasn't Ended for Gig Economy Workers," *Vox*, May 28, 2019, http://www.vox.com/policy-and-politics /2019/5/28/18638480/gig-economy-workers-wellbeing-survey; and Charlotte Jee, "Coronavirus Is Revealing the Gig Economy's Sharp Inequalities," *MIT Technology Review*, March 12, 2020, http://www.technologyreview.com/s/615350 /coronavirus-covid19-gig-economys-sharp-inequalities-tech-business/.

15. Eduardo Porter, "Tech Is Splitting the U.S. Work Force in Two," *New York Times*, February 4, 2019, http://www.nytimes.com/2019/02/04/business /economy/productivity-inequality-wages.html.

16. David Autor and Anna Salomons, "Is Automation Labor-Displacing? Productivity Growth, Employment, and the Labor Share," *Brookings Papers on Economic Activity: BPEA Conference Drafts, March 8–9, 2018*, February 27, 2018.

17. S&P Dow Jones Indices, "S&P 500 Buybacks Up 3.2% in Q4 2019; Full Year 2019 Down 9.6% from Record 2018, as Companies Brace for a More Volatile 2020," *PR Newswire*, March 24, 2020, http://www.prnewswire.com/news-releases /sp-500-buybacks-up-3-2-in-q4-2019-full-year-2019-down-9-6-from-record-2018 --as-companies-brace-for-a-more-volatile-2020--301028874.html.

18. Jonathan Krieckhaus et al., "Economic Inequality and Democratic Support," *Journal of Politics* 76, no. 1 (2013): 139–151, http://www.jstor.org/stable/10.1017/s0022381613001229.

19. Jennifer McCoy, Tahmina Rahman, and Murat Somer, "Polarization and the Global Crisis of Democracy: Common Patterns, Dynamics, and Pernicious Consequences for Democratic Polities," *American Behavioral Scientist* 62, no. 1 (2018): 16–42, http://doi.org/10.1177/0002764218759576.

20. Michael H. Goldhaber, "Attention Shoppers!" *Wired*, December 1, 1997, http://www.wired.com/1997/12/es-attention/.

21. Zahra Vahedi and Alyssa Saiphoo, "The Association between Smartphone Use, Stress, and Anxiety: A Meta-Analytic Review," *Stress and Health* 34, no. 3 (2018): 347–358, http://doi.org/10.1002/smi.2805.

22. Edward Bullmore, *The Inflamed Mind: A Radical New Approach to Depression* (New York: Picador, 2019).

23. Nicholas Carr, *The Shallows: What the Internet Is Doing to Our Brains* (New York: W. W Norton, 2020).

24. Steve Lohr, "It's True: False News Spreads Faster and Wider. And Humans Are to Blame," *New York Times*, March 8, 2018, http://www.nytimes.com/2018/03/08/technology/twitter-fake-news-research.html; and Ana P. Gantman, William J. Brady, and Jay Van Bavel, "Why Moral Emotions Go Viral Online," *Scientific American*, August 20 2019, http://www.scientificamerican.com/article/why-moral-emotions-go-viral-online/.

25. Eric Meyerson, "YouTube Now: Why We Focus on Watch Time," *YouTube Official Blog*, August 10, 2012, http://youtube-creators.googleblog.com/2012/08/youtube-now-why-we-focus-on-watch-time.html.

26. Conor Friedersdorf, "YouTube Extremism and the Long Tail," *Atlantic*, March 12, 2018, http://www.theatlantic.com/politics/archive/2018/03/youtube-extremism-and-the-long-tail/555350/.

27. Caroline O'Donovan et al., "We Followed YouTube's Recommendation Algorithm down the Rabbit Hole," *BuzzFeed News*, January 24, 2019, http://www.buzzfeednews.com/article/carolineodonovan/down-youtubes-recommendation-rabbithole; and Manoel H. Ribeiro et al., "Auditing Radicalization Pathways on YouTube," *Proceedings of the 2020 Conference on Fairness, Accountability, and Transparency* (2020): 131–141.

28. Guillaume Chaslot, "How Algorithms Can Learn to Discredit 'the Media,'" *Medium*, February 1, 2018, http://medium.com/@guillaumechaslot/how-algorithms-can-learn-to-discredit-the-media-d1360157c4fa.

29. Chaslot.

30. Andy Greenberg, "WhatsApp Comes under New Scrutiny for Privacy Policy, Encryption Gaffs," *Forbes*, February 21, 2014, http://www.forbes.com

/sites/andygreenberg/2014/02/21/whatsapp-comes-under-new-scrutiny-for
-privacy-policy-encryption-gaffs.

31. "Google Organic CTR History." Advanced Web Ranking, updated February 2021, www.advancedwebranking.com/ctrstudy/.

32. Katy Waldman, "Facebook's Unethical Experiment," *Slate*, June 28, 2014, http://slate.com/technology/2014/06/facebook-unethical-experiment-it-made
-news-feeds-happier-or-sadder-to-manipulate-peoples-emotions.html.

33. Robert M. Bond et al., "A 61-Million-Person Experiment in Social Influence and Political Mobilization," *Nature* 489, no. 7415 (2012): 295–298, http://doi.org/10.1038/nature11421; and Carole Cadwalladr, "'I Made Steve Bannon's Psychological Warfare Tool': Meet the Data War Whistleblower," *Guardian*, March 18, 2018, http://www.theguardian.com/news/2018/mar/17
/data-war-whistleblower-christopher-wylie-faceook-nix-bannon-trump.

34. Jeffrey H. Dryer, Hal Gregersen, and Clayton M. Christensen, "The Innovator's DNA," *Harvard Business Review*, December 2009, http://hbr.org/2009/12
/the-innovators-dna.

35. Levi Boxell, Matthew Gentzkow, and Jesse M. Shapiro, "Cross-Country Trends in Affective Polarization," *National Bureau of Economic Research* (2020), http://doi.org/10.3386/w26669.

36. Michael Sainato, "The Americans Dying Because They Can't Afford Medical Care," *Guardian*, January 7, 2020, http://www.theguardian.com/us-news
/2020/jan/07/americans-healthcare-medical-costs.

37. Samuel L. Dickman, David U. Himmelstein, and Steffie Woolhandler, "Inequality and the Health-Care System in the USA," *Lancet* 389, no. 10077 (2017): 1431–1441, https://doi.org/10.1016/S0140-6736(17)30398-7.

38. K. Robin Yabroff et al., "Prevalence and Correlates of Medical Financial Hardship in the USA," *Journal of General Internal Medicine* 34 (2019): 1494–1502, https://doi.org/10.1007/s11606-019-05002-w.

CHAPTER 9

1. Hannah Ritchie and Max Roser, "Technology Adoption," Our World in Data, 2017, https://ourworldindata.org/technology-adoption. Data source: Diego A. Comin and Bart Hobijn and others, "Technology Adoption in US Households," *Our World in Data*, 2004, latest data update July 27, 2019, http://ourworldindata.org/grapher/technology-adoption-by-households-in-the-united-states.

2. Arielle Pardes, "This Dating App Exposes the Monstrous Bias of Algorithms," *Wired*, May 25, 2019, http://www.wired.com/story/monster-match
-dating-app/.

3. Office of the Privacy Commissioner of Canada. "WhatsApp's Violation of Privacy Law Partly Resolved after Investigation by Data Protection Authorities," January 28, 2013, news release, http://www.priv.gc.ca/en/opc-news/news-and -announcements/2013/nr-c_130128/.

4. Dino Grandoni, "WhatsApp's Biggest Promise May Get Broken with Facebook Deal," *HuffPost*, March 10, 2014, http://www.huffpost.com/entry /facebook-whatsapp-privacy_n_4934639.

5. Dave Lee, "Amazon's Next Big Thing May Redefine Big," BBC News, June 15, 2019, http://www.bbc.com/news/technology-48634676.

6. Commonwealth of Massachusetts v. Purdue Pharma L.P., et al. First Amended Complaint and Jury Demand, Civil Action No. 1884-cv-01808 (BLS2), January 31, 2019, http://www.mass.gov/files/documents/2019/01/31 /Massachusetts%20AGO%20Amended%20Complaint%202019-01-31.pdf.

7. Milton Friedman, "A Friedman Doctrine—the Social Responsibility of Business Is to Increase Its Profits," *New York Times*, September 13, 1970, http://www.nytimes.com/1970/09/13/archives/a-friedman-doctrine-the-social -responsibility-of-business-is-to.html.

8. Francesco Guerrera, "Welch Condemns Share Price Focus," *Financial Times*, March 12, 2009, http://www.ft.com/content/294ff1f2-0f27-11de-ba10 -0000779fd2ac.

9. Dominic Rushe, "Deepwater Horizon: BP Got 'Punishment It Deserved' Loretta Lynch Says," *Guardian*, October 5, 2015, http://www.theguardian.com /environment/2015/oct/05/deepwater-horizon-bp-got-punishment-it-deserved -loretta-lynch-says.

10. Jim Morrison, "Air Pollution Goes Back Way Further Than You Think," *Smithsonian*, January 11, 2016, http://www.smithsonianmag.com/science-nature /air-pollution-goes-back-way-further-you-think-180957716/.

11. Simon Caulkin, "Ethics and Profits Do Mix," *Guardian*, April 19, 2003, http://www.theguardian.com/business/2003/apr/20/globalisation .corporateaccountability.

12. Daniel H. Pink, *Drive: The Surprising Truth about What Motivates Us* (Edinburgh: Canongate, 2018).

13. James K. Rilling et al., "Opposing BOLD Responses to Reciprocated and Unreciprocated Altruism in Putative Reward Pathways," *NeuroReport* 15, no. 16 (2004): 2539–2243, http://doi.org/10.1097/00001756-200411150-00022.

14. Daeyeol Lee, "Game Theory and Neural Basis of Social Decision Making," *Nature Neuroscience* 11 (2008): 404–409.

15. Joseph Adamczyk, "Homestead Strike," *Encyclopædia Britannica*, updated March 4, 2020, http://www.britannica.com/event/Homestead-Strike; and Christopher Klein, "Andrew Carnegie Claimed to Support Unions, but Then Destroyed

Them in His Steel Empire," History.com, July 29, 2019, http://www.history.com /news/andrew-carnegie-unions-homestead-strike.

16. Benjamin I. Page, Larry M. Bartels, and Jason S. Wright, "Democracy and the Policy Preferences of Wealthy Americans," *Perspectives on Politics* 11, no. 1 (2013): 51–73, http://doi.org/10.1017/s153759271200360x.

17. Klaus Schwab, "Davos Manifesto 2020: The Universal Purpose of a Company in the Fourth Industrial Revolution," World Economic Forum, December 2, 2019, https://www.weforum.org/agenda/2019/12/davos-manifesto-2020-the -universal-purpose-of-a-company-in-the-fourth-industrial-revolution/.

18. Jim Loehr, "4 Rules to Craft a Mission Statement That Shapes Corporate Culture," *Fast Company*, May 8, 2012, http://www.fastcompany.com/1836576 /4-rules-craft-mission-statement-shapes-corporate-culture.

19. Luisa Beltran, "WorldCom Files Largest Bankruptcy Ever," CNN Money, July 22, 2002, http://money.cnn.com/2002/07/19/news/worldcom_bankruptcy/.

20. Wikipedia, s.v., "Enron Code of Ethics," last modified December 13, 2020, 00:49, https://en.wikipedia.org/wiki/Enron_Code_of_Ethics.

21. Hilary Andersson, "Social Media Apps Are 'Deliberately' Addictive to Users," BBC News, July 4, 2018, http://www.bbc.com/news/technology -44640959.

CONCLUSION

1. Monetary Authority of Singapore and industry contributors, *Principles to Promote Fairness, Ethics, Accountability and Transparency (FEAT) in the Use of Artificial Intelligence and Data Analytics in Singapore's Financial Sector*, updated February 7, 2019, https://www.mas.gov.sg/~/media/MAS/News%20and%20 Publications/Monographs%20and%20Information%20Papers/FEAT%20 Principles%20Final.pdf.

2. Betsy Beyer et al., eds., *Site Reliability Engineering: How Google Runs Production Systems* (Sebastopol, CA: O'Reilly, 2016).

3. Margaret H. Hamilton, "What the Errors Tell Us," *IEEE Software* 35, no. 5 (September/October 2018): 32–37, 2018, https://doi.org/10.1109 /MS.2018.290110447.

4. Browder v. Gayle, 142 F. Supp. 707 (M.D. Ala. 1956), https://catalog .archives.gov/id/279205.

INDEX

Page references followed by *f* indicate an illustrated figure; those followed by *t* indicate a table.

ABOUT THE AUTHOR

Radhika Dutt is an entrepreneur and product leader and has participated in four acquisitions, two of which were companies that she founded. She is currently advisor on product thinking to the Monetary Authority of Singapore, Singapore's financial regulator and central bank. She also teaches entrepreneurship and innovation at Northeastern University's D'Amore-McKim School of Business and is an advisor to several startups. Dutt cofounded Radical Product Thinking as a movement of leaders creating vision-driven change and is a frequent speaker at business events and conferences around the world. She graduated from MIT with a bachelor's degree and a master's degree in electrical engineering, and speaks nine languages, currently learning her tenth.

Dutt started her first company while still at MIT—she cofounded Lobby7, a venture-backed company that created an early version of Siri back in 2000. Lobby7 was acquired by ScanSoft/Nuance. She later worked at Avid, growing its broadcast business by building a product suite for digital media that transformed how broadcasters put news on the air. She then led strategy at the telecom startup Starent Networks—Starent was Cisco's largest acquisition at the time. She then started Likelii, offering consumers "Netflix for wine" until Likelii was acquired by Drync. Following the acquisition, she led product management at

Allant to build a SaaS (software as a service) product for TV advertising; Allant's TV division was acquired by Acxiom for the product that she built.

Dutt has a uniquely varied background in that every job she has held has been in a different industry. She has built products in industries including broadcasting, media and entertainment, advertising technology, government, consumer apps, telecommunications, and robotics. Her journey into product leadership made her realize that "product" is a way of thinking that can be applied almost anywhere, not only a job title or function. Just as sales is a life skill that's useful in a job interview, product thinking is a life skill for creating change in the world around you.

Berrett–Koehler
Publishers

Berrett-Koehler is an independent publisher dedicated to an ambitious mission: *Connecting people and ideas to create a world that works for all.*

Our publications span many formats, including print, digital, audio, and video. We also offer online resources, training, and gatherings. And we will continue expanding our products and services to advance our mission.

We believe that the solutions to the world's problems will come from all of us, working at all levels: in our society, in our organizations, and in our own lives. Our publications and resources offer pathways to creating a more just, equitable, and sustainable society. They help people make their organizations more humane, democratic, diverse, and effective (and we don't think there's any contradiction there). And they guide people in creating positive change in their own lives and aligning their personal practices with their aspirations for a better world.

And we strive to practice what we preach through what we call "The BK Way." At the core of this approach is *stewardship,* a deep sense of responsibility to administer the company for the benefit of all of our stakeholder groups, including authors, customers, employees, investors, service providers, sales partners, and the communities and environment around us. Everything we do is built around stewardship and our other core values of *quality, partnership, inclusion,* and *sustainability.*

This is why Berrett-Koehler is the first book publishing company to be both a B Corporation (a rigorous certification) and a benefit corporation (a for-profit legal status), which together require us to adhere to the highest standards for corporate, social, and environmental performance. And it is why we have instituted many pioneering practices (which you can learn about at www.bkconnection.com), including the Berrett-Koehler Constitution, the Bill of Rights and Responsibilities for BK Authors, and our unique Author Days.

We are grateful to our readers, authors, and other friends who are supporting our mission. We ask you to share with us examples of how BK publications and resources are making a difference in your lives, organizations, and communities at www.bkconnection.com/impact.

Dear reader,

Thank you for picking up this book and welcome to the worldwide BK community! You're joining a special group of people who have come together to create positive change in their lives, organizations, and communities.

What's BK all about?

Our mission is to connect people and ideas to create a world that works for all.

Why? Our communities, organizations, and lives get bogged down by old paradigms of self-interest, exclusion, hierarchy, and privilege. But we believe that can change. That's why we seek the leading experts on these challenges—and share their actionable ideas with you.

A welcome gift

To help you get started, we'd like to offer you a **free copy** of one of our bestselling ebooks:

www.bkconnection.com/welcome

When you claim your **free ebook**, you'll also be subscribed to our blog.

Our freshest insights

Access the best new tools and ideas for leaders at all levels on our blog at ideas.bkconnection.com.

Sincerely, pt rule

Your friends at Berrett-Koehler

Certified

Corporation